THE NORFOLK DIALECT

Further details on these titles can be found at
www.poppyland.co.uk
where clicking on the 'Support and Resources' button
will lead to pages specially compiled to support this title

The Norfolk Dialect

Peter Trudgill

POPPYLAND PUBLISHING

First published 2003
ISBN 0 946148 63 5

Published by Poppyland Publishing, 4 Alfred Road, Cromer NR27 9AN

Picture credits
All photographs are from Poppyland Photos except for that of Sidney Grapes (p. 14), which is reproduced by permission of Keith Skipper.

Designed and typeset in 9½ on 12 pt Arial by Watermark,
Cromer, NR27 9HL

Printed by Printing Services (Norwich) Ltd

Contents

To the memory of my father, John Trudgill,
who drew this picture of Westlegate, Norwich
(see page 24)

Acknowledgements

I have had invaluable help from a number of people in writing this book, including especially David Britain and Jean Hannah, who I am very grateful to. Warm thanks are due, too, to Stuart Bowell, Peter Brooks, Neil Brummage, and Norman Hart.

In preparing this text, I have inevitably drawn on my own experience of the Norfolk dialect. I was born in Thorpe St Andrew, Norwich, in 1943. I went to the City of Norwich School, and then to Cambridge and Edinburgh Universities. At Edinburgh I wrote my Ph.D. thesis which later appeared as a Cambridge University Press book called *The Social Differentiation of English in Norwich*. This was based on analyses I made of tape-recorded interviews I carried out with 60 people in Norwich during the summer of 1968. If any of them read this book, I would like them to know that I remain very grateful to them for their cooperation and patience and help. I derived a lot of my knowledge of the local dialect from them.

Perhaps even more important, however, was what I learnt from my own family. I was lucky enough to have two grandparents, George Gooch and Jane Fish, who were native speakers of the North Norfolk rural dialect; and two, George Trudgill and May Carver, who spoke the Norwich form of the dialect. I dedicate this book to their memory. I have also had very helpful discussions over the years about the Norfolk dialect with my uncle, Ken Gooch. And most of all, I am especially grateful to my mother, Hettie Trudgill, for the help I have received from her and the insights she has given me.

INTRODUCTION

This book is intended to be an introduction to the dialect of the English county of Norfolk, both for those who already know it and love it and for those who do not. It looks first at the linguistic history of the county, and of all the many different languages which have been spoken there, in an attempt to see what influences may have contributed to the distinctive nature of our dialect. Then we take a look at the dialect of Norfolk in the context of the English dialects of Great Britain as a whole. We will see that, not surprisingly, there are very many similarities between our dialect and those of neighbouring areas, notably Suffolk. However, geographical proximity is not necessarily the only factor involved. One of the most important dialect boundaries in the whole of Britain is the one that passes through the Fens, and there are many respects in which the speech of Norfolk is much more similar to that of, say, Hampshire, 200 miles away than to that of our immediate neighbours in Lincolnshire. The next chapter deals with the vocabulary of the Norfolk dialect. Here we shall see that there are very few words that belong to Norfolk exclusively and that what is distinctive about our dialect is the particular combination of words that are used locally.

There is a brief description of the grammatical structure of the Norfolk dialect – the way that words are made up of smaller grammatical units and the way in which words are combined into sentences. We can have a lot of fun using the Norfolk dialect, but, like all varieties of English, Norfolk is also a dialect which is worthy of respect and which has a dignity of its own. I have respected its dignity here, and in other chapters, by using the same sort of serious, academic linguistic terminology to describe the Norfolk dialect that I would use to describe any other language or dialect in the world. I know that not all readers will be familiar with all of this terminology, so I have tried to give examples of what I mean so that people can work out what I am talking about even if they have never seen a particular term before.

We will be explicitly or implicitly comparing the grammar of our dialect to the grammar of Standard English. Standard English is the dialect of English which is normally used in writing, which is normally taught in schools, and which is generally taught to foreigners learning English. Standard English differs from the other, nonstandard dialects of the English-speaking world in a number of ways. In Standard English, the past tense form of the verb *to do* is *did* – *I did it yesterday* – while in nearly all other dialects it is *done* – *I done it yesterday* – and Norfolk is no exception. Standard English does not allow more than one negative form in a phrase – *I couldn't see any anywhere* – whereas other dialects, including Norfolk (and many foreign languages), do allow this – *I couldn't see none nowhere.*

Nonstandard dialect forms, including Norfolk dialect forms, are often considered to be 'mistakes'. It is often said to be 'wrong' to say *I done it*. This is most definitely not the case. There is nothing wrong with saying *I done it* as such (although if you said this in the belief that you were speaking Standard English, you *would* be wrong). The grammar of the Norfolk dialect is not 'wrong'; it is just different from that of Standard English. All dialects and languages have grammatical rules, and this is quite naturally true of Norfolk also. For example, if someone who wanted to learn the Norfolk dialect noticed that Standard English *did* can correspond to Norfolk *done* and therefore said **Done you go last night?,* this would be wrong. For reasons that I will give in chapter 4, it would be a mistake because it would be breaking one of the grammatical rules of our dialect. (Note that I use the symbol * to show that a form is non-existent.)

It is quite true that Standard English has more social status and prestige and influence than other dialects, but that does not make it 'correct'. Traditionally, people who spoke Standard English were more powerful, wealthy and educated than people who spoke only the Norfolk dialect; they also tended to come from the capital city, London, or near to it, which gave their language more prestige. But that does not make the Norfolk dialect, or any other dialect, less worthy in any way. Of course, being able to write Standard English does confer social advantages, which is why we teach it in our schools. But there is nothing magical about the grammar or the vocabulary of Standard English which makes it better than other forms of English.

As to whether people should speak Standard English or not, I always feel uncomfortable about recommending people to do so if they have not grown up speaking in this way. It is true that many in our society are bigoted against regional dialects, and dialect speakers can be discriminated against. But we do not say to people who suffer from racial or sexual discrimination that they should change their race or sex; and I think it is important to point to discrimination against regional dialect speakers as the unpleasant prejudice that it is and to try and remove it as far as possible.

One of the points of this book is to show that the Norfolk dialect is a form of the English language with a fascinating history and a unique structure that is worthy of respect and maintenance, not of ridicule and discrimination. Our local dialects of the English language are not some haphazard collection of erroneous deviations from the standard norm which are due to ignorance or laziness. On the contrary, Standard English *grew out of* the dialects; and the Norfolk dialect was particularly influential in the development of the English language in Britain (and beyond, as we shall see on pages 92–5). London was the capital city of England, and Standard English gradually emerged from the form of English spoken there, the London dialect. This London dialect was in origin very much a mixed dialect because of the heavy in-migration to the capital from other parts of the country, and especially from areas of southeastern England that were close to it, notably East Anglia, with Norfolk being very well represented. The point is therefore that there is nothing special about Standard English, linguistically speaking. If the capital of England had been in Newcastle rather than London, then there is no doubt that Standard English would have grown up out of a mixture of dialects from the northeast instead of the southeast of England, and we would today have been writing things like *I is* rather than *I am* and *He's ganging* rather than *He's going.*

Then there is a chapter looking at the pronunciation of the Norfolk dialect. It is not always easy to portray on the printed page the way a dialect sounds, particularly to those readers who have never heard it before. Such readers may therefore have to work a bit harder than they, and I, would like in order to understand what I am trying to convey – obviously nothing can beat actually hearing the dialect as it is spoken. Again, in this chapter we will implicitly and explicitly be comparing the pronunciation of the Norfolk dialect with other forms of English, and I will often use the term 'General English' here and in other chapters to refer to varieties of English other than the Norfolk dialect.

THE NORFOLK DIALECT

All languages change through time. We do not really know why this is, but it is a characteristic of all human languages. They also change in different ways in different places. This is why we can start off with a single language like West Germanic (see pages 20–24) and end up 2,000 years later with different languages such as English, German and Dutch. It is also the reason why we have different dialects. We will note on pages 70–91, for instance, that the pronunciation of the Norfolk dialect differs from that of other dialects, sometimes because changes have taken place in Norfolk which have not taken place elsewhere, and sometimes because Norfolk has been more conservative and not adopted changes that have occurred elsewhere.

This constant process of change is a little bit of a problem for this book. One of the oldest records we have of the Norfolk dialect is the book by Rev. Robert Forby called *The Vocabulary of East Anglia* which I will refer to a number of times in the rest of this book. His book was published in 1830, and it is obvious that the Norfolk dialect has changed a lot since that time. It is also clear to anyone over the age of, say, 40 who has lived in Norfolk all their lives that the dialect continues to change. It would be easy to hark back to a time when elderly people spoke the 'pure' or 'real' Norfolk dialect and to feel that this has in more recent times been 'corrupted' and that it is 'dying out'. But we have to remember that Forby might very well have thought of the speech of even the most conservative dialect speakers we can remember today as being 'corrupted'. In the early nineteenth century

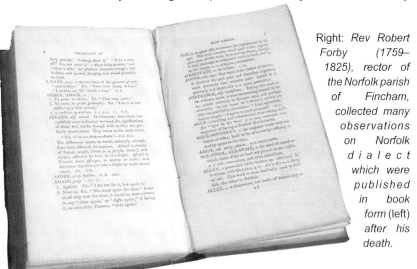

Right: *Rev Robert Forby (1759–1825), rector of the Norfolk parish of Fincham, collected many observations on Norfolk dialect which were published in book form* (left) *after his death.*

speech described by Forby, the Norfolk dialect had pronunciations such as *char* 'chair', *dar* 'dare', *fudder* 'further', *hash* 'harsh', *mell* 'mill', *fram* 'from', *funt* 'font', *deed* 'dead', *brumm* 'broom', *tow* 'tough', *fow* 'few'. Very few people alive today, if any at all, have ever heard such pronunciations. Our dialect is a living form of speech, and like all dialects it continues, and will continue, to change. I have recognised this in the text by using terms like 'older' and 'traditional' versus 'modern' and 'more recent'. And I have tried to record not just the dialect of older country people but also that of younger urban speakers.

In the early 1970s I had a very interesting conversation with Eric Fowler, who wrote in the *Eastern Daily Press* under the name of Jonathan Mardle and who was a leading authority on the Norfolk dialect. He loved the older, rural way of speech which he perceived to be disappearing and regretted the dialect of Norwich, which he regarded as 'ugly'. I did not agree. I was not able to change his mind about this, unfortunately, but I still hold to the view that if we want a distinctively Norfolk form of English to survive, then we have to encourage and support all varieties of our local dialect, including especially that of the city. There are more people in Norwich than any other single place in Norfolk, and if the Norwich dialect does not survive, then there is little hope for the more rural forms.

It is true that we can see the influence of London English making itself felt in Norfolk – younger people now often say *fing* and *bruvver* rather than *thing* and *brother*. But this spreading of language forms from one place to another has always happened: the pronunciation of *v* as *w*, as in *willage* for *village*, which we now think of as being a distinctively Norfolk dialect form (see page 84), undoubtedly spread to Norfolk from London in the 19th century, and only later became thought of as a local dialect feature because it died out in London before it did here. And it is encouraging to notice that the influence can also go the other way: I suggest on pages 92–5 that a number of features of Norfolk pronunciation may in more recent times have spread or be spreading outwards to other areas.

In writing this book, I have drawn on the work of others, notably Forby, mentioned above, and the dialect writing in Sidney Grapes' *The Boy John Letters,* which represent a body of Norfolk dialect work of not a little genius. The letters were written to

Sidney Grapes in character as 'the Boy John'.

and published in the *Eastern Daily Press* between 1946 and 1958, and a selection was later published in a booklet entitled *The Boy John.* Sidney Grapes was the proprietor of a bicycle shop, later a garage and motor business, in Potter Heigham, a village in the northeast Norfolk Broadland district. In the years before the Second World War, he acquired a reputation as an amateur Norfolk dialect comedian, performing at social functions in many parts of the county and on the radio. The letters appeared in the newspaper at irregular intervals – Grapes would simply write them when he felt like it – and were always signed 'The Boy John'. They purported to be reports of events in the Boy John's village, and, in addition to the Boy John – a farm worker himself – they featured as their main characters his Aunt Agatha, Granfar, and old Mrs W—, their neighbour. Most of the letters ended with a PS containing one of Aunt Agatha's aphorisms, which became famous throughout the county, such as 'Aunt Agatha she say: all husbands are alike, only they have different faces so you can tell 'em apart.' Not only were the characterisations and vignettes of village life brilliant – and therefore enormously popular – but Sidney Grapes was also, by common consent, a superb writer of the local dialect, right down to subtleties such as Granfar speaking in a more conservative, traditional way than the other characters. The spelling system he used for the dialect was rather variable, even to the extent of spelling the same word in two different ways in the same letter, but it was always accurate within the framework of the conventions he was working with.

One of the most attractive features of *The Boy John Letters* is their humour. The sense of humour that accompanies the Norfolk dialect is not at all like that associated with the Cockney of London or the Scouse of Liverpool, though perhaps it is not so very different from the humour of some other predominantly rural areas. Norfolk humour is 'dry', slow, deadpan, controlled, sardonic, understated, ironic, teasing. This is not always understood by outsiders – which is part of its point. In his 1927 book *In Search of England*, H. V. Morton describes the following incident:

> I was lost in a Norfolk lane, so I stopped a man and I said to him: 'Good morning!' He looked at me. 'Good morning,' I cried. 'Can you tell me if I am right for Norwich?' He continued to look at me. Then he said : 'What d'ye want to know for?' I might have been annoyed, but leaning out of the car and putting on an affable expression which I usually keep for tea-parties, I said: 'My dear old bor, I want to know because I want to get to Norwich.' The ghost of a smile flitted over his rustic face, and he replied after some deep thought, rather reluctantly, and looking away from me: 'Well, you're right!'

Morton interprets this behaviour on the part of the Norfolkman as being due to a distrust of outsiders, in a rather isolated part of the country, and he even remarks that the Norfolkman behaved 'in an uneasy, suspicious way'. I think most Norfolk people would have an entirely different interpretation of what happened. Here is a rather patronising, supercilious outsider, driving a car at a time when very few people had one, who is being teased by the local 'peasant' and is not clever enough to realise it.

THE LINGUISTIC HISTORY OF NORFOLK

Personal introduction

When I was nearly five years old, my parents took my brother and me, and my maternal grandparents, on holiday to Eccles on the east coast of Norfolk. We lived in Norwich so it was not very far, but it seemed a long way to me, and many new and exciting things about Eccles have stuck in my mind ever since. One is the ruins of the mediaeval church on the beach which was being eaten away, as much of the Norfolk coast is, by the sea. Fifty years later it is no longer there.

Another was the name of the village itself. I remember thinking it was strange. I was (I now imagine) used to place names like Barningham, where my grandparents lived, and those of seaside resorts such as Sheringham and Waxham; and to names such as those of other seaside places like Morston and Bacton and Winterton. And I also knew of other seaside places with comfortable sounding names like Hemsby, Scratby and Ormesby. But Eccles sounded funny.

Little did I know then that there was a good reason why it sounded funny. Names ending in *ham* were coined by my linguistic and, I have to suppose, genetic ancestors who came over the North Sea around AD 450 and who brought with them forms of speech which were soon to turn into Old

English, which is the historical ancestor of Modern English. *Ham* in their language meant 'home', and Sheringham is so called because it was the home of the *ing* – that is, the 'people' – of Scira. The *ton* names come from *tun,* which in their language meant 'enclosure' or 'homestead'. The equivalent word in modern German, *Zaun,* means 'fence'; and in modern English it has become *town*. Winterton meant the village where the local people lived in the winter (Somerton, where one of my great-great-grandfathers came from, is just down the road).

Hemsby, on the other hand, is a rather newer name. Hemsby was the village of a Viking leader called Hemer, and it was founded and named by Norsemen who crossed the North Sea about 400 years later. The word *by* was and still is the Scandinavian word for 'settlement' (in modern Norwegian it means 'town', in Swedish 'village'*)*. Like most people from eastern England, I probably have Viking blood in my veins too.

But Eccles is different. It is a much older name. It was there before the arrival of Scira and his people from across the North Sea, and well before that of Hemer and his followers. What does Eccles mean? One clue comes from the ruined church on the beach which so fascinated me as a child: Eccles means 'church'. But what language is this name from, if it is not Old English or Scandinavian? The answer is that it is a word in a language which was once spoken all over Norfolk and indeed all over Britain. One indication as to what language it was comes from the name of another seaside place, just north of Eccles, which is also rather unusual, even though it is Old English in origin: Walcott. It is perhaps not too surprising to discover, if we think of the word *cottage*, that the *cott* bit at the end of this village name means 'dwelling'. But what does *Wal* mean? Perhaps somewhat surprisingly, it means 'Welsh'. Walcott was 'the dwelling of the Welsh'. The people who lived all over Norfolk at the time of the arrival of the Anglo-Saxons were the Welsh, and Eccles, the name of a place which is just about as far from Wales as it is possible to get in England today, is a Welsh-language place name corresponding to the modern Welsh word for 'church', *eglwys*.

The Celts

Strictly speaking, the language that was spoken in Norfolk for perhaps a thousand years until about AD 500 was not Welsh as such but its Celtic ancestor, Brythonic or British. This was also the ancestor of Cornish and of Breton, the Celtic language still spoken today in Brittany by the descendants of Celts who escaped from the Anglo-Saxons across the English Channel from Devon and neighbouring areas. This Celtic language had no real influence on modern East Anglian dialects. This is hardly surprising, in view of the fact that it came under threat from Old English so early on in this part of the world.

Astonishingly, however, Claxton in his book *Suffolk Dialect* tells us of a report in the *East Anglian Magazine* that shepherds in the Leiston area of Suffolk in the 19th century counted sheep in a way which is certainly at least partly Celtic in origin. Here are the numbers they used, compared to the modern Welsh equivalents:

	Suffolk	**Welsh**
1	unna	un
2	tina	dau
3	wether	tri
4	tether	pedwar
5	pinkie	pump
6	hater	chwech
7	skater	saith
8	sara	wyth
9	dara	naw
10	dick	deg

At least the numbers for 1, 4, 5 and 10 seem related (*pump* is pronounced 'pim' or 'pimp'), and probably also 2. There are many other reports of similar counting systems from elsewhere in the country. In some places they are reported as having also been used in children's counting games – the rhymes in the Suffolk list are typical. Many of these reports come from Cumbria, where a form of Welsh known as Cumbrian was still spoken in mediaeval times. It would be amazing to think that a Welsh-based counting system was still remembered in East Anglia 1400 years after the language which it originally came from had died out there, but we cannot be sure that it was not a later reintroduction from somewhere else.

A number of place names in Norfolk have also been retained from the time when Welsh was the main language of the area. The *Lynn* of King's Lynn, for example, is from early Welsh *lindo* 'pool', which in modern Welsh is now *llyn* 'lake'. This is thought to be because the original settlement at Lynn was situated by a pool at the mouth of the river Ouse. The word *Ouse* itself is also Celtic, being related to the Scots Gaelic *uisge* 'water', which in the form *uisge beath* 'water of life' is the origin of the word *whisky*. And the name of the river Yare, which in Old English was called *Gerne*, is probably also from a Celtic root *ger-* or *gar-* which meant 'babbling river'. Loddon derives from the British name for the river Chet, which was *Lutna* 'muddy river'. The names of North and South Creake are related to Old Welsh *creic*, modern Welsh *craig* 'hill', which was borrowed into English as *crag*. And Trunch – a very un-English sounding name – may be from British *trun ceto* 'promontory wood', where *ceto* corresponds to modern Welsh *coed* 'wood'. There is also another Eccles near Attleborough.

The Romans

East Anglia had come under Roman control by AD 47, but the British language continued to be spoken by the famous East Anglian Iceni tribe of Boudica, and the other Celtic groups in Britain, throughout the Roman occupation, which lasted for four hundred years or so.

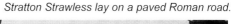

Stratton Strawless lay on a paved Roman road.

In spite of the fact that we have to suppose many people became bilingual to varying degrees in Brythonic and Latin during the occupation, the language of the Romans has left few traces in Norfolk. The place-names Caister (near Yarmouth), Caistor St Edmunds (near Norwich), and Brancaster go back to Latin *castra* 'military camp'. And Stratton Strawless, Long Stratton and Stradsett have names which go back to Latin *stratum* 'paved road' (Long Stratton lay on the Roman road, the modern Norwich-Ipswich road, which led to Caistor St Edmund).

The birth of English

The English language which replaced Welsh in Norfolk and, subsequently, in much of the rest of Britain, is today most closely related historically to three other modern languages: German, Dutch and Frisian. We say that these languages are 'related' because they are all descended from a common parent language which we now call West Germanic. We know that West Germanic was spoken in what is now the Netherlands, northern Germany and southern Denmark about 2,000 years ago, and we have a good idea of what it was like, even if we have no written records of it.

If, therefore, we were to ask when English first came into being as a language, what we would really be asking would be when it started breaking away from the other West Germanic languages, and especially from Frisian, which is its closest relative. Frisian is still spoken today in Friesland, the northern part of the Netherlands. It was long recognised as being a language rather similar to English, and East Anglian fishermen had a rhyme which went:

> Bread, butter and green cheese
> Is good English and good Friese.

The Frisians, too, still have a version of the same rhyme:

> Bûter, brea en griene tsiis
> Is goed Ingelsk en goed Fries.

A reasonable answer to the question of when English began to separate from the other West Germanic dialects and acquire its own identity is the following. English started existence as an independent language when

The pedlar of Swaffham, famous in folklore – here seen on the end of a pew in Swaffham church.

speakers of West Germanic, who had originally crossed the North Sea from mainland Europe as raiders and mercenaries during the Roman occupation, first started to overwinter, and then settle permanently, in Britain. These people were members of the tribal groupings we now refer to as the Angles, Saxons, Jutes and Frisians. They came mainly from coastal districts just across the North Sea from Britain. The Jutes came from the furthest north, in southern Denmark. The Angles lived in areas to the south of them, with the Saxons still further to the south, on the coast of northern Germany. The Frisians lived furthest to the south, on what is now the Dutch coast. Other smaller West Germanic groups were also involved in the invasion and colonization: Swaffham was originally *Swaefasham*, which meant 'home of the Swabians', and most of this tribe eventually ended up in southwestern Germany.

It was, then, the permanent settlement of these people in eastern Britain that was eventually to lead to the break-up of the West Germanic dialects into separate languages and to the development of the English language. East Anglia was, of course, immediately across the North Sea from the coastline of the original area occupied by these West Germanic peoples, and it was therefore one of the very first British areas where they settled. We can therefore say that East Anglia was one of the earliest English-speaking places in the world, if not the very first place. It is quite possible, in other words, that the English language was actually born in Norfolk.

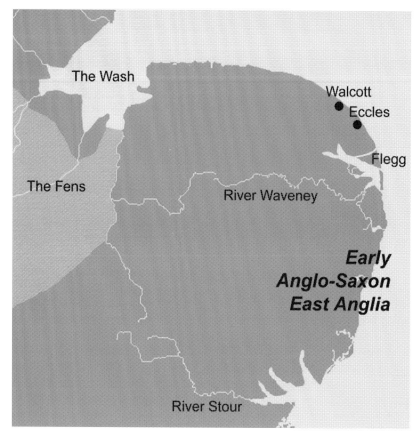

Map 1: Anglo-Saxon and Danish East Anglia

The birth of the Norfolk dialect

Most of the West Germanic people who settled in Norfolk were Angles, but there was probably also a sizeable Frisian element. The Angles and the Frisians were the people who formed settlements in Norfolk with names ending in *-ham, -ton,* and *-ing.* And these were the people who caused the disappearance of Welsh from our area, although they learnt and carried on using some Welsh river names, as we have seen. Welsh-speakers either gradually merged with the Germanic invaders, giving up their language in the process – the presence of names such as Walcott suggests that Celtic and Germanic peoples did live alongside one another at least for a while – or they fled to the west. The early Welsh language is known to have survived in the Fens longer than elsewhere in eastern England, until perhaps AD 650.

The form of the English language that was spoken in England and southeastern Scotland from the time of the arrival of the West Germanic peoples until about 1100 is called Anglo-Saxon or, more correctly as we saw above, *Old English*. The modern Norfolk dialect descends from the Old English which grew out of the Anglian dialects that were brought over the sea from Europe during the 5th century AD. East Anglia was probably a distinctive dialect area from the very beginning. The Angles arrived in England via the Wash. Some then turned east, and others north. The ones who turned east were to become known in England as the Eastern Angles. Groups of Saxons, on the other hand – the ones later to be known as the East Saxons – also arrived via the Wash but headed south along the Ouse and the Icknield Way, occupying Cambridgeshire and Essex, as well as areas further west – Middlesex, Huntingdon, Hertfordshire and Bedfordshire. Norfolk and Suffolk, then, were mainly Anglian, and the areas which bordered them to the south and west – Essex and Cambridgeshire – were distinct from the very beginning by reason of being mainly Saxon. Regional differences in eastern England in language and customs thus simply reflected different areas of origin in mainland Europe. The expert on East Anglian place names, O. K. Schram, believed that the Kingdom of East Anglia – modern Norfolk and Suffolk – constituted a single, mainly Anglian ethnic and linguistic unit from very early on, and he suggested that it is not a coincidence that Norfolk and Suffolk both have towns or villages called Barningham, Barsham, Brettenham, Elmham, Fakenham, Helmingham, Ingham, Needham, Rougham, Shimpling, Thornham, Tuddenham and Walsham. The kingdom, once it became established, was probably bordered in the south by the river Stour and in the west by the Ouse, the Lark and the Kennett, thus leaving the Newmarket and Haverhill areas, from a modern perspective, on the 'wrong' side of the border (see Map 1). The kingdom, however, later expanded further west, for a time, up to the River Cam.

It is also known that at a quite early period the Norfolk and Suffolk dialects became somewhat different from one another. It is difficult today to imagine the rivers that separate Norfolk and Suffolk, the Little Ouse and the Waveney, forming any kind of barrier to communication, but 1500 years ago things would have been different. The name Waveney itself comes from *wagen-ea*, which meant 'quagmire-river', and we have to suppose that Norfolk and Suffolk were divided from one another by land that was marshy and difficult to cross, and that the dialect differences which developed reflected a relatively low level of contact across those rivers.

Tombland, an open place in Danish times, overlooked by the Norman cathedral.

The Danes

The Anglian-origin English of Norfolk developed gradually, with little outside influence, for about four hundred years. Then, however, as we saw above, the Vikings arrived. The ones who arrived in Norfolk were mostly Danes. The Great Viking Army of 865 successfully invaded much of East Anglia, and this area became officially part of the Danelaw – the area of England which was signed over to the Danes by King Alfred in a treaty from about 890 onwards. Many settlers, mostly farmers, arrived from Denmark after this; and Thetford, in particular, became a mainly Viking town. In spite of the fact that Norfolk and Suffolk soon came back under English control – some time in the early 900s – the influence of the Danish language remained considerable, indicating that large numbers of Danes must have stayed in the area. Danish certainly continued to be spoken in East Anglia for two hundred years or more before its speakers, too, gradually abandoned it in favour of English. One reason why this abandonment was so slow is perhaps that Danish is a Scandinavian language, and its original parent language, North Germanic, was a close relative of West Germanic. It is therefore quite probable that English speakers and Danish speakers could still understand one another and communicate reasonably well during the 9th and 10th centuries without changing one language for another.

Since the Angles had already occupied many of the most productive areas of land, Danes often settled in places which were less desirable in some way. Flegg, in eastern Norfolk, for example, was an island surrounded by marshes – the name is the same word as *flag*, i.e. 'iris', and probably meant 'reeds'. It was heavily settled by Danes, as is shown by the presence of place-names ending in *by*, as we mentioned before. In addition to the names cited above, there are Ashby, Clippesby, Billockby, Oby, Herringsby, Mautby, Thrigby, Rollesby, Filby, and Stokesby. Other Danish place names in East Anglia are those including *thorpe* and *toft*. Thorpe, as in Ashwellthorpe, is a Danish word referring to an outlying smaller village which was dependent on a *by*. Toft, as in Lowestoft, means 'dwelling site' – in modern Danish it still means 'paddock' or 'croft'. The Danish word for street was *gate,* which we still find in names such as Pottergate and Westlegate in Norwich. And Tombland, in Norwich, comes from the Danish word *tom*, which means 'empty'.

The Normans

After the Norman conquest in 1066, Norwich itself, by now a rather sizeable town, must have been a very multilingual place. In addition to the original speakers of English and, for 200 years or so, Danish, there would have been, obviously, speakers of the newly arrived Norman French. The Normans also brought with them from the continent large numbers of speakers of other languages, especially Flemish (Dutch), from the Low Countries, and Breton (a relative of Welsh, as we saw earlier) from Brittany. It is astonishing to think of Tombland in Norwich alive with people speaking as many as five different languages. Later, during the 14th century, there were also numerous additional Flemish-speaking weavers who arrived in the city. Norman French, also known as Anglo-Norman, survived as a spoken language in England until the 14th century.

The Jews

Many Jews also arrived with the Normans, and subsequently. They were probably mostly speakers of French and would have remained so for the most part until they were expelled from Britain in the 13th century. They would also have had a knowledge of Hebrew as their liturgical language and language of scholarship and literature. There was a sizeable community in Norwich living in the area between what is now the Haymarket and the Back of the Inns. One of the most famous mediaeval Jewish poets lived in Norwich and wrote in Hebrew. He is known to Jewish scholars today as Meir ben Elijah of Norwich.

The Romany

The Romany arrived in Britain in the late middle ages. They were called 'Gypsies' because it was erroneously thought that they had come from Egypt. In fact, their origins were much further away than that, in northwestern India. It is not known why they left India, but it has been suggested that they were escaping from the constraints of the caste system. They spread rather slowly through Afghanistan, Iran and the Middle East. Some arrived in Spain and Portugal via North Africa. Others moved into Europe via the Balkans.

Their language is originally a north Indian language and is related to Hindi, Punjabi, and other languages of the area. George Borrow, the Norfolk writer who was born in Dereham, spent some time with groups of Romany – on Mousehold Heath in Norwich, for example – and it is clear from his descriptions in books such as *Lavengro* and *Romany Rye* that the Romany in Norfolk still spoke their own language in the 19th century. Borrow claimed to have learnt to speak it. Today, however, Romany is no longer spoken in England, though some families in Wales are said to retain it. The language survives rather well in many other countries, though, including Romania, Hungary and Slovakia, as well as the United Sates. What is left in Britain is a form of speech called Anglo-Romany. This is a kind of in-group slang which is essentially English in grammar and pronunciation but with Romany words. A number of words from Anglo-Romany have come into modern English, including *pal, cosh,* and *moosh* 'mate' (as a term of address).

The Strangers

Perhaps the most dramatic influx of other languages into Norfolk, again from across the North Sea, happened in the 16th century. In 1565, the mayor and aldermen of Norwich had invited 30 'Dutchmen' and their families – no household was to exceed ten persons – to Norwich in an attempt to modernise the local textile industry, which was of great economic importance to the region, but which had been lagging behind in terms of technology, design and skills. In the event, 24 Flemish and 10 Walloon master textile makers arrived and settled in Norwich. Then, some years later, following religious persecution at the hands of the Spanish Inquisition, Protestant refugees of Dutch, Flemish and Walloon (French-speaking) origin fled from the Low Countries, now Belgium and The Netherlands, which were then under Spanish control, to England. Some settled in Sandwich (Kent), London and Colchester. However, by far the biggest group of refugees found its way to Norwich, probably attracted at least in part by the already established group of invited weavers there.

The refugees themselves, although predominantly textile workers, included ministers, doctors, teachers, merchants and craftsmen. They were mostly Dutch speakers from Flanders and Brabant, but there were also many French-speaking Walloons from Armentières, Namur and Valenciennes (at this period, the border with France was further south than it is today), and even some German speakers from Lorraine. The very high proportion of 'Strangers', as they were called, in the city did lead to a certain amount of friction, and there was at least one attempted revolt against them; but generally, the absorption of a very large number of refugees into the population, while it undoubtedly caused overcrowding, seems to have been relatively trouble-free. By 1579, 37% of the population of Norwich, which at that time was 16,236, were native speakers of Dutch or French rather than English!

Some of the Flemish-speaking community returned to the Low Countries, ironically as a result of religious persecution, during the 1600s, but the

foreign community was further strengthened by the arrival of some French Huguenots after the revocation of the edict of Nantes, which had promoted religious tolerance, in 1685. According to the Norfolk historian R. W. Ketton-Cremer, church services in Dutch and French were maintained in the churches in Norwich that had been given over to the immigrant communities 'for many decades', and the congregations seem to have remained vigorous until 1700 or so. (The Walloon church on Queen Street can still be visited.) The last French-language service in Norwich was in 1832, and the last one in Dutch, in Blackfriars Hall, in the 1890s, although by then the languages had attained

The Walloon church in Norwich.

the status of liturgical languages only. It is clear, however, that Norwich remained a trilingual city for 200 years or so, well into the 18th century.

The Dutch influence on Norfolk is clear from the presence in Norwich and other Norfolk towns of open areas which are not called *squares*, as they would be elsewhere, but *plains*, from Dutch *plein* – in Norwich we have Bank Plain, St Andrews Plain, and so on, and in Sheringham there is *Lifeboat Plain*. We will discuss Dutch influence further on pages 37–8.

Recent history

In more recent centuries, the Norfolk dialect survived well as a distinctive variety, sheltered to a certain extent from outside influence by its relatively remote position and poor transport connections. Since the Second World War, however, just as the East Anglian dialect area as a whole has been getting progressively smaller as London forms spread outwards, so Norfolk is now in a much weaker position than formerly. Increasing in-migration from the Home Counties and 'the Sheers' – the counties to the west of East Anglia which, unlike Norfolk, Suffolk and Essex, have names ending *shire* – as well as London overspill housing schemes in Thetford and King's Lynn, have proportionally reduced the demographic base of Norfolk dialect speakers. Nevertheless, happily, reports of the death of the Norfolk dialect have been greatly exaggerated.

THE PLACE OF NORFOLK AMONG ENGLISH DIALECTS

The traditional English dialects of Britain are divided into two major geographical subgroups, those of the North and those of the South (see Map 2). The dialects of the North are those of Scotland, the English northeast, Cumbria, and north and east Yorkshire. The South is subdivided into two large areas, Central and Southern. The Central dialects are those of Lancashire, South and West Yorkshire, and the Midlands – places where people pronounce *up* as 'oopp' and *dance* as 'dannse', for example.

Norfolk is obviously therefore a dialect from the Southern area. The Southern dialect area is divided into a Western and an Eastern subgroup. The Western area stretches from Cornwall to Kent, and from southern Shropshire via Berkshire to Sussex. It is in this area that dialect speakers pronounce the *r* in words like *car* – 'carr'.

The Eastern dialects – and Norfolk is obviously one of these – are divided into two main areas, the Central East and East Anglia. The Central East area consists of the central and eastern parts of Northamptonshire, parts of Bedfordshire and Buckinghamshire, Cambridgeshire, non-metropolitan parts of Hertfordshire, and most of Essex. The East Anglian area thus covers northeastern Essex, Suffolk and Norfolk and is therefore rather bigger than it was in Old English times. Among the East Anglian dialects, Norfolk forms a distinctive, separate area.

As a result of these different levels of division and subdivision of English dialects, the geographical borders of the Norfolk dialect area have different degrees of importance. In the west, just to the south of the Wash in the Fens, there is a very clear and important dialect boundary, as we noted earlier. This boundary, which coincides with the county line and the river Nene, is the major boundary between the Southern (East Anglian – Norfolk) and the Central (Eastern Central – Lincolnshire) dialect areas. On the A17, Terrington St Clement is Southern, Norfolk-speaking, while as soon as you cross into Sutton Bridge you will hear people saying 'boot-

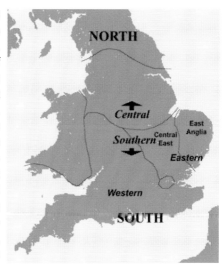

Map 2: English dialects

ter, oopp, coopp' for *butter, up, cup*, in the Central or Midlands dialect manner, and notice that boys are called *lads*. The Norfolk dialect is thus the northernmost of all the southern dialects of England.

The river Nene at Sutton Bridge – boundary between two major dialect areas.

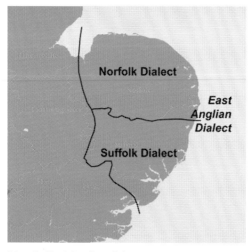

Map 3: East Anglian dialects

A little further to the south, the western dialect boundary is less dramatic, since it is a boundary with another Southern and indeed Eastern dialect area, the Central East. Interestingly, the boundary here does not coincide exactly with the county boundary. Some people in the Norfolk Fens speak the Central East dialects more typical of Wisbech, Cambridge and Northampton rather than Norfolk. Upwell, Emneth, West Walton, the Walpoles and Outwell, although actually in the county of Norfolk, are Central Eastern speaking. On the other hand, Clenchwarton, Terrington St John, Marshland, St John's Fen End, Downham Market, the Tilneys and Nordelph are all Norfolk speaking. This is because the Fens were mainly uninhabited until relatively recently, and when they were drained, people moved in from the west, south and east. The location of the modern dialect boundary reflects the extent to which people moved in from the originally inhabited areas of Norfolk, crossing the Ouse and heading towards the Nene, rather than from elsewhere.

The southern boundary, between the Norfolk and Suffolk dialect areas, is even less significant, since they are both part of the East Anglian area and the dialects are very similar. Nevertheless, there are plenty of differences between the two. For example, splinters are called *shivers* in Norfolk, *slivers* in Suffolk. A snail is known as a *dodman* in Norfolk, a *hodmedod* in Suffolk. And the term *left couch* 'left-handed' is confined to Norfolk. The dialect boundary between Norfolk and Suffolk coincides mostly with the county boundary and thus with the line of the Little Ouse and the Waveney. Unlike in the Old English period, however – no doubt as a result of the decline of the importance of the Waveney as a barrier – much of northeastern Suffolk is basically Norfolk rather than Suffolk speaking. Beccles, Bungay and Lowestoft are certainly Norfolk speaking, and we can probably say the same for places as far south in Suffolk as Halesworth and Southwold. These are places which 'look to' Norwich (and where people mostly support

Norwich City Football Club rather than Ipswich Town), and the location of the dialect boundary reflects the relative historical influence of Norwich and Ipswich as urban centres (see map 3).

The Norfolk dialect area is of course not uniform, either. There are differences between the northeast, northwest, southwest and southeast of the area. Gorse is known as *whinbush* in western Norfolk but *furbush* (or *furrabush)* in the east. A mould-board on a plough is called a *plat* in northern Norfolk but a *breast* in the south. And the urban dialects of Norwich, King's Lynn, Yarmouth/Gorleston and Lowestoft all have their own distinctive characteristics.

Oulton Broad and Lake Lothing (above) *and Lowestoft harbour* (below) *are still within the Norfork dialect area, though both sides of the waterway are administratively in the county of Suffolk.*

THE VOCABULARY OF THE NORFOLK DIALECT

The idea of a 'Norfolk dialect word' is rather problematic. We like to talk of 'Norfolk words', of course, but it is actually impossible to find words which are truly 'Norfolk' in the sense that they are found in all of Norfolk and only in Norfolk. As we just saw, there are some words, like *whinbush* and *furbush,* which are found only in parts of the county. Then there are many other words which are found in all of the county but cannot be claimed as truly Norfolk words since they also occur in Suffolk and/or Cambridgeshire – and so on. It is true that, as mentioned in the previous chapter, there are cases such as splinters being called *shivers* in Norfolk and *slivers* in Suffolk, but we also have to remember that the dialect boundary between Norfolk and Suffolk dialect is not the same as the county boundary, so that the 'Norfolk' word is also found in what is officially, from a local government point of view, Suffolk.

The concept of a 'dialect word' is also a difficult one. Many lists of Norfolk words actually include words which are found all over the country, such as *pightle* 'small field or enclosure'. Such words are sometimes considered to be dialect words because knowledge of them is confined to people who have worked in or are close to the older agricultural world, and they are therefore unknown to townspeople and to younger people generally. But we cannot really claim them for Norfolk.

Other apparently dialect words are simply retentions of usages which have died out in General English, such as *to allow* 'admit', *nigh* 'near', *forenoon* 'morning', and *howsomever* 'however'.

Similarly, some so-called 'dialect words' are basically general English words but with a distinctive local pronunciation. *Trosh'n* is not really a Norfolk dialect word as such; it is simply the General English word *threshing* with a distinctive Norfolk pronunciation. So is *troshel* 'threshold'. *Blar* 'cry' is a local form of *blare,* the word *duzzy* 'foolish' is our variant of *dizzy* (which comes from Old English *dysig* 'foolish'), and *brotch* or *brawtch* 'open' is simply our way of saying *broach.*

Sometimes words we think of as being local are not local at all: *squit*, meaning 'nonsense', may not be known to Londoners, but it is known and used in the dialect of Herefordshire, which is about as far away from Norfolk as you can get and still be in England. Then there are historical problems to do with regional origins. Knowledge of the word *mawther* 'girl' may be more or less confined to Norfolk these days, but the English Dialect Dictionary shows that it used to be known and used in Suffolk, Essex, Cambridgeshire and Hertfordshire as well. And our local dialect word *harnser* 'heron' was a word that, in the form *heronshaw* 'young heron', was formerly known all over the country, as was *tempest* 'storm'.

Whinbush, or furbush.

And there are also words which are known all over the country but which we tend to use more in Norfolk than other people do, such as *hull (hurl)* for 'throw', *reckon* for 'think, believe',* and *rum* for 'strange', as in the famous Norfolk phrase *'Ass a rumm'n! '*That's a funny thing!' Sometimes, too, it is simply the usage which is different: the words *boy* and *girl* are General English words, but in Norfolk we have the distinctive custom of using them as terms of address – *Come you on boy!* – or as terms of reference to particular, adult people: *the boy John, the gal*

Mary. We are also fonder than most other people of using the adjective *old* to indicate familiarity or disparagement: *Thass oony an ol' sparra* 'It's only an old sparrow'; *Thass a lot a old squit* 'It's a lot of nonsense'. And when we greet somebody by saying *Are y'alright?,* we are not asking after their health, merely greeting them.

Origins

Some of our local vocabulary can be traced back to the multilingual history of the region.

Danish

Very many General English words indeed are of Scandinavian origin. Words which arrived as a result of the Viking invasions include: *egg, skirt, sky, disk,* and scores of others including *they, them* and *their.* In parts of Britain where Danish or Norwegian influence were especially strong, even more Scandinavian words from the Old Norse language spoken by the Vikings survive in local speech. This is particularly true of Scotland, the Lake District, and Yorkshire. As a result of our Danish heritage, the Norfolk dialect, too, has a

Scarrow Beck.

number of words of Danish origin which, while they may not be confined to Norfolk, are not part of the general vocabulary of English. For example, *beck* 'stream' is of Danish origin. The word *staithe,* meaning 'landing stage', is also Danish, as are *carr* (Old Norse *kjarr)* 'bog overgrown with brushwood', and *marram* 'sea grass' – the modern Danish word is *marehalm*, which literally means 'sea reed'.

Many people will be surprised to know that the word *bairn* 'child' was still in use in Norfolk in the 1930s – the modern Danish word for child is *barn*. *Dag* 'dew' is Scandinavian – the modern Norwegian word is *dogg* – and so is *dow* 'dove, pigeon'. *Grup* 'small trench, often at the side of the road' would seem to be the same word as Norwegian *grop* 'pothole'. And while in Norfolk we do not have the Scandinavian-origin north-country word *lig* 'to lie', we do have *ligger*, which is a plank laid across a dyke used as a bridge. The word *paddock, pudd* 'toad' is related to Scandinavian *padde*. And *stroop* 'throat' is the same as modern Norwegian *strupe*, with the same meaning.

French

The Walloons, the French-speaking Strangers, seem to have left relatively little influence behind them, though the word *lucam* 'attic window' is probably from French *lucarne* 'skylight'. This is particularly likely since the word referred to the upper windows where weavers used to sit and work to get the best light – and very many of the Strangers were weavers, as we have seen.

Dutch

The issue of Dutch influence is more difficult to determine. As mentioned earlier, Dutch and English are closely related languages which both descended from West Germanic. Resemblances between Dutch and forms of English are therefore most usually due not to the influence of Dutch on English, or vice versa, but to their common origin. We cannot say that English *house* 'comes from' Dutch *huis* but rather that both *house* and *huis* are descended from the same West Germanic word, *huus*. Nevertheless, when we find English words that resemble Dutch and that are found *only or mainly* in East Anglia, then it is worth considering whether or not they derive from close contact across the North Sea, or from the Flemish speakers who arrived with the Norman conquest, or from the Flemish weavers who arrived in the 14th century, or from the massive numbers of Dutch-speaking Strangers who arrived in the 16th century

– we have already noticed the presence of *plains* rather than *squares* in Norfolk towns in this connection.

Words which may very well be of Dutch origin include the following. *Dwile* 'floorcloth' seems rather obviously to come from Dutch *dweil,* which has the same meaning. *Crowd* 'to push, as of a wheelbarrow or bicycle' may very likely have come from Dutch *kruien* 'to push a wheelbarrow'. *Deek*, meaning 'dyke, ditch', is probably from Dutch *dijk.* And *fye out* 'clean up' may well be connected to Dutch *vegen* 'to sweep', while *push* 'boil, pimple' is probably derived from Dutch *puist* 'pimple'. The word *foisty* 'mouldy, musty' is basically the same word as *fusty*, and may derive from Dutch *fust* 'cask'; this is also the same word as French *fût,* Old French *fust.*

Other languages

The word *cooshie* 'a sweet' is probably the same word as *cushy* 'soft, easy, as of a job' which is said to come from the north Indian language Hindi, where *khush* means 'pleasant'. This would then be one of a number of words brought back from India by British soldiers.

English

Other local dialect words are words which were found in Old English but which are now confined to our region or have acquired special meanings in our dialect. The famous Norfolk general term of address, *bor*, which according to Forby, is applied indiscriminately to persons of both sexes and all ages, comes from Old English *bur* or *gebur*, which meant 'farmer'. This is the same form which is found in *neighbour*, which comes from Old English *neah bur* 'near-farmer'. In modern Dutch *buur* means 'neighbour'.

To fare 'to seem' is from Old English *faran* and is basically the same word as general English *fare*, as in *he didn't fare very well*, but with a special Norfolk meaning. *To hain* 'to raise, heighten' is from Old English, and so is *fang* 'catch hold of' – the modern German word *fangen* means 'to catch'. *Pishameer* 'ant' and *pollywiggle* 'tadpole' are also Old English words.

Other words

Here is a brief list of some other Norfolk words.

ah the Norfolk equivalent of *aye* 'yes'. It is generally used to agree with somebody:

> *Thass cold today.*
> *Ah, that is!*

rather than in answering yes-no questions such as *Are you a-comen*?, where *yes* would be more usual as a positive answer. No-one knows what the origins of *aye* are. It is not known to be an Old English word, and it was first recorded as late as the 16th century.

a-thawt across. A form of *athwart*. *Thwart* is from an Old Norse word, and *tvert* in modern Norwegian still means 'crosswise'.

to betty about to fuss around, probably from the woman's name Betty.

bigotty awkward, socially difficult. This, obviously, comes from the word *bigot*, which is originally of French origin.

bishybarnybee 'ladybird, Bishop Bonner's bee'. Bishop Bonner, from Dereham, was a ferocious burner of protestant martyrs during the reign of Queen Mary.

blee resemblace. Also a verb *to blee* 'resemble'. From Old English *bleo* 'colour, hue', which by Middle English had become a poetic word only, meaning 'complexion, visage', and later, by extension, 'appearance'. The word has been obsolete in General English since about 1600, but was alive and well in Norfolk until quite recently.

to blow to boast, brag. This metaphorical usage of *blow* was at earlier times found outside Norfolk also.

boke bulk. In *The Boy John Letters* we can read 'Wen yow city and town people ride trew tha country yow'll notis our stacks arnt so big this year; tha's acos the straw earnt so long, as Granfar say, "There earnt a lot a boke ter year".'

caddow   jackdaw. Normally pronounced *cadda*. The *–dow* part seems to be the same as the *–daw* part in *jackdaw, dawe* in Old English meaning 'a small bird of the crow type'. The *ca-* part is from an old word meaning 'jackdaw'.

carnser   causeway over a marsh. A from of *causeway,* from the Old North French *caucee.*

cockey   dyke, stream. There were several cockeys in Norwich. Since they were used to carry off sewage, when they were covered over the word came to mean 'sewer, drain'. Part of London Street in Norwich used to be known as Cockey Lane because of a stream, the Great Cockey, which ran alongside; it started in what is now the Surrey Street area, and ran via the Back of the Inns into the

Cockey Lane in Norwich follows the course of a small stream.

Wensum just west of St Georges Street. Schloars are agreed that the *–ey* part of this word probably comes from Old English *ea*, river, the same word which appears in the name of the River Waveney, mentioned earlier, and the River Wissey. The *cock-* part is much more difficult. The Swedish expert on the place-names of Norwich, Karl Inge Sandred, tells us that origins in Celtic *kok* 'water channel', Old English *cocc* 'gully', and Old Norse *kók* 'gullet' have all been proposed, but that none is really satisfactory.

couch   *left couch* and *couch handed* both mean 'left-handed'.

doon   noise, sound. This word is usually found in negative sentences, e.g. *He never made a deen.* It appears to be a form of *din*, which comes from the Old English *dynn*. However, the Norfolk pronunciation suggests that our dialect word may actually come from the related Old Norse word *dynr*, compare the modern Faroese *dynur* 'noise, din'.

dene   sandy area by the coast. Unlike *dune,* this word can refer to a flat area of sand as well as hillocks. The origin is uncertain, but it seems to be a form of an Old Germanic word, originally borrowed from Celtic as *dūn*, also

South Denes, Yarmouth.

giving modern English *dune* and *down* (as in the South Downs).

dickey   donkey. The original English word for donkey was *ass*, but this became too embarrassing for some people when pronunciation changes in the language made *ass* a possible pronunciation of *arse*. This led to a whole number of euphemisms being used, all of them derived from men's names. *Donkey* comes from *Duncan*. A Scottish word for donkey is *cuddy*, which comes from *Cuthbert*. The  children's word *Neddy* is from *Edward*. And our own *dickey* is, of course, from *Richard*.

dockey   farmworkers' midmorning snack or lunch. We do not really know what the origins of this word are, but it may be related to *dock*, meaning 'cut' or 'reduce', the implication perhaps being that pay would be docked for time taken off for eating.

dodman   snail. The origins of this word are not really known. However, it has been suggested that it may be related to a little-known word *dod*, meaning a bare, rounded hill-top, which comes from a Middle

English word *dodden*, 'to make the top of something bare', as in de-horning cattle. (Note that the English from the mediaeval period is known by scholars as *Middle English*.)

to drant	to drawl, drone. A dialect word found in East Anglia and Scotland. It appears to be onomatopoeic, i.e. imitative of the sound in question in origin.
to draw	to move slowly. Also in the form *to drawlatch*.
drift	trackway down onto the marshes (from the *driving* of cattle).
to dudder	to shiver. This is a local form of *dither*, which originally meant 'to tremble'. The old Norfolk dialect, as described by Forby, had a number of words in which *th* in the middle had become *d*. In the Introduction I mentioned *fudder* 'further'; and we know that *Southery* in the Fens used to be pronounced *Suddery*.
duller	noise. Also a verb meaning 'to make a noise' as in *Do you stop that dulleren!* Probably from *dolour*, 'pain, grief, anguish', hence, originally, 'a mournful noise'. *Dolour* was originally pronounced *duller*, and comes from Latin *dolere* 'to grieve' via French, compare modern French *douleur*.
dwainy	weak, sickly. There was an Old English word *dwinan* which meant 'to waste away' which became *to dwine* in Middle English. This form has disappeared as such, but survives in the form of *dwindle*. The Norfolk word may come from the Old English form, or it may be from a related early Modern Dutch word *dwijnen* 'to vanish'.
fit	ready, as in *Are ya fit?*
to garp	to stare, probably a form of *gape*.
gays	pictures in a magazine etc., illustrations. This usage obviously relates to the adjective *gay*, which was originally the French word *gai*. The meaning 'picture in a book' is

attested from different parts of England from the 1600s.

hake	hook over a cooking fire, pothook. The General English word *hook* derives from Old English *hōc* 'hook'. *Hake*, on the other hand comes from the related Old Norse word *haki*, also meaning 'hook', and/or from the Dutch word for 'hook' *haak*. Even if we no longer have pothooks, some people remember this word in the simile 'as black as a hake'.
holl	a hollow, dip in the ground. This is the Old English word *hol*, Middle English *holl*, related to *hole* and *hollow*. In Old English it could also mean 'cave'.
horkey/hawkey	harvest festival or supper. The *Oxford English Dictionary* say the origins of this word are 'unknown'.
huh	*on the huh* means 'not straight'.
hulver	holly, from Old Norse *hulfr.*
hutkin	finger protector, literally 'a little hut'.
to jam on	to step on (e.g. someone's foot).

loke   narrow lane. This is from the Old English *loca* 'an enclosed place', and may be related to *lock.*

mardle   talk, gossip, chat. Some people have related this word to another dialect word *mardle*, meaning 'pond', presumably on the grounds that this was originally the sort of chat you would have by the village pond, but this is doubtful.

mavish song thrush. *Mavis*, originally a French word, was formerly the general word for this bird.

mawkin scarecrow. This is derived from *Mal*, an abbreviated form of the woman's name *Matilda*, or from *Maud*, plus the diminutive suffix *-kin*. In some parts of England the form *malkin* is found.

mawther girl; also *mauther*. As a term of address, it can be abbreviated to *maw*. This was formerly the word for 'girl, young woman' in all the Eastern Counties including Hertfordshire. The neutral meaning 'girl' seems in more recent times to have been partly replaced by a less favourable meaning 'large awkward girl', and in this meaning it has been reported as far away as Gloucestershire. The origins of this word have puzzled linguists and philologists greatly. We are fairly certain that it has no connection with *mother*. It may be related to *maid*, which is an abbreviated form of *maiden*, from Old English *mægden*. The original meaning of *maid* was 'girl', and it is still used in this meaning in some West Country dialects.

milches the soft roe of male fish. This is a form of *milt*, which is an old West Germanic and North Germanic word meaning 'spleen'.

million pumpkin, often in *million pie* 'pumpkin pie'. A form of *melon*. There is an older attested form of *melon*, *millon*, from which the Norfolk form is most likely to derive.

mob to scold, nag. This obviously derives from the word *mob* 'unruly crowd', which is an abbreviation of Latin *mobile vulgus* 'excitable crowd'. In most of the English-speaking world, therefore, it requires a large group of people to 'mob' somebody. In Norfolk, though, you can do it all by yourself.

ought nought, as in *Norwich City won six-ought,* from the Old

45

English word for 'anything'.

peevish   malicious, spiteful. This word seems to have first appeared in English about 1500. Its origins are not known. The Norfolk usage represents an older meaning which is now obsolete elsewhere. In General English the word now means 'irritable'.

pit   pond. The same word as General English *pit*, but note the closer connection with the original meaning: the word descends from Old English *pytt*, which meant 'a well'. The meaning of 'hole in the ground for water' became obsolete in areas other than Norfolk in about 1600.

quant   punt. Perhaps this is from Latin *contus,* from the Ancient Greek *kontos* 'boat pole'. This word is general in East Anglia and Kent.

ranny   shrew. According to the *Oxford English Dictionary,* this word is 'apparently from the Latin *araneus mus* "spider mouse".'

raw   cross, angry. An extended meaning of *raw*.

relly   also *rally.* A narrow ledge or shelf built into a wall.

rudle   weak tea. Originally a joking reference to the pale colour of tea which is not strong enough. *Rudle*, more usually known as *ruddle* outside Norfolk, was a 19th-century drink consisting of a mixture of warm beer, gin, and sugar, with a slice of lemon peel.

smur   drizzle. A dialect word found in East Anglia and Scotland. The origin is not known.

sosh   *on the sosh* means 'not straight'.

sowpig   wood louse; also *sowbug.*

spink   finch, especially chaffinch. Formerly used in many parts of England. The origin of this word is not known, but it may well be imitative of the sound of the bird-call.

stam to amaze. From an old word *stam* meaning 'a state of bewilderment', which is probably from the Old English adjective *stamm* 'stuttering'.

stingy cruel, malicious. In General English this word means 'mean, ungenerous', but is seems that the Norfolk dialect preserves the original meaning. (Note the same sort of relationship between English English *mean* 'ungenerous' and American English *mean* 'malicious'.) The word may derive from *sting*.

swift a newt. This is an Old English name, derived from the adjective meaning 'quick', presumably in reference to the rapid movements of this small amphibian. *Swift* is an Old English word which is probably related to *swoop*. The word *newt* itself was in Old English *eft* or *ewt*. The modern form of the word is the result of a re-division: *an ewt > a newt*.

swimmer a Norfolk dumpling, so called because it floats in gravy.

tizzick cough. Also *tissick, tisick*. A word that appears in Shakespeare. It comes from *phthisic* 'tuberculosis', from the Ancient Greek for 'to waste away'.

totty small. Derived from *tot*, which is a rather new word, first recorded in 1725, in the meaning of 'small child'. *Totty* as an adjective seems to be confined to our dialect.

to tricolate decorate. The Norfolk dialect poet John Kett writes, in his poem *An Ordinerry Rood*, that flowers
. . . mark all the passin' seasons, that they dew,
An tricolate right well that windin' way'.

wem also *wame.* An imperfection, such as a stain on a piece of clothing. From Old English *wam* 'spot, blemish', which became Middle English *wem* 'defect (including moral defect), injury, stain'. The word has been obsolete in General English for centuries, but was alive and well in Norfolk in living memory.

THE GRAMMAR OF THE NORFOLK DIALECT

As we said earlier, all dialects have grammatical rules – it is simply the case that the rules of particular dialects differ from the rules of Standard English. In this chapter we look at the grammatical rules of the Norfolk dialect - the rules which have to do with the way in which words and sentences are composed - and point out differences between the grammar of our dialect and the grammar of Standard English.

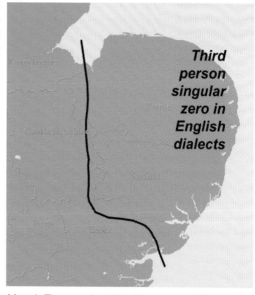

Third person singular zero in English dialects

Verbs

3rd person singular forms

Standard English has a simple present tense verb system like this:

Map 4: The area in which 'He go crazy' is a normal way of speaking.

singular	plural
I run	*we run*
you run	*you run*
he/she/it runs	*they run*

The 3rd person singular form – the 'he/she/it' form – is irregular in that it has an additional *-s*. Middle English did not have an *-s* here but rather *-eth* or *-th*, as in *my cup runneth over*. This earlier form is still familiar to us from, for example, the King James version of the Bible and from Shakespeare. Northern dialects of English, however, never had this *-th* but rather *-s*, or *-es* or *-is*. During the 15th century, for reasons we do not fully understand, this originally northern form started spreading south and by the 1500s had made its way into colloquial London English, though upper-class and formal speech still used the original *-th*. Shakespeare, writing in the late 1500s and early 1600s, used both *-th* and *-s* forms depending on which of his characters was speaking and how formal the situation was. Now the *-th* form has completely disappeared, although it lingered on in the traditional dialects of Devon and Cornwall until the early years of the 20th century.

In Norfolk, however, as in the rest of East Anglia, while the *-th* disappeared, it was replaced not by the newer, originally northern *-s* form. It was replaced by nothing at all – so we can call it a 'zero' form. The Norfolk present tense verb system is therefore like this:

singular	plural
I run	*we run*
you run	*you run*
he/she/it run	*they run*

It is a characteristic of the Norfolk dialect that we say:

> *He say . . .*
>
> *She go . . .*
>
> *He like her very much. – Oh, do he?*

This is a very sensible verb system since the *-s* of Standard English is redundant – it plays no role in communicating meaning since it is always clear that the verb is 3rd person from the subject (*he, she* etc.). The area of England including Norfolk where the traditional dialects have this system is shown in Map 4. It is not just a feature confined to the traditional dialect, however, but lives on very strongly today in modern Norfolk speech, including that of Norwich and Yarmouth.

One interesting question is why East Anglia is the only area of Britain to have this system. (Other areas either have the Standard English system with third-person singular *-s*, or else – in parts of the north and west of England – have the 'new' *-s* for all persons: *I goes, we likes* etc.) My own theory about this is that it has to do with the 'invasion' of Norwich in the 16th century by the remarkable group of people known as the Strangers, people we would today call refugees or asylum seekers. As we saw, they were mostly native speakers of Dutch (Flemish), but there was also a good proportion of speakers of French.

People who are learning English as a foreign language often have trouble with the unpleasantly irregular 3rd-person singular *-s* of Standard English. This well-known fact results, for example, in stereotyped foreigners such as Manuel in the BBC TV series *Fawlty Towers* saying things like 'He go crazy!' My explanation, then, is that the more or less simultaneous arrival into Norwich of *he likes* from the north of England, and *he like* from the foreigner English of the Strangers, both in competition with the old *he liketh*, led to a situation where there was a sort of competition between the three forms; and that, in this competition, the most regular form was the one which eventually won. It then subsequently spread outwards from Norwich, which was the second largest city in England at the time, to the whole of the area which it dominated culturally and economically, namely East Anglia.

a-verbing

In addition to the simple present tense, the English language also has a continuous present tense, as in *I am running, you are running, she is running* etc. In the Norfolk dialect it is usual for the participle form ending in *–ing* to be preceded by *a-*, as in *I'm a-runnen*. (The *–ing* part is normally pronounced '-en' in Norfolk, so that *taking* and *taken* are pronounced identically.) This is a feature of very many English dialects, in the United States as well as Britain, and is rather well known to most people in the English-speaking world from folk-songs and other similar sources. It preserves *a-*

from a much older period of the language when the *-ing* forms were nouns – as they can still be, as in *I like running* – and when people said things like *I am at running,* i.e. engaged in running as an activity.

This original history of the *–ing* verb forms as nouns can still be seen from the fact that in Norfolk, transitive verb forms (i.e. verbs with objects) are normally followed by *on* (which corresponds to Standard English *of*):

He wus a-hitten on it.	= He was hitting it.
I'm a-taken on em.	= I'm taking them.
What are you a-doen on?	= What are you doing?

Continuous versus simple verb forms

The Norfolk dialect sometimes uses simple verb forms where other dialects would use continuous forms with *-ing*:

The kittle bile!	= The kettle's boiling!
I go to Norwich tomorra.	= I'm going to Norwich tomorrow.
The wind blow!	= The wind is blowing.

Irregular verbs: past tense forms and past participles

English has two types of verb, regular and irregular. Regular verbs, by far the biggest class, are those like *love* which have only two main forms and where the past tense form and the past participle – the form used with *have* to form the 'perfect' – both take *-ed*:

I love   I loved   I have loved

Irregular verbs are those which do not take *-ed* and where the past tense form and the past participle are often different in form, giving three main forms:

I see   I saw   I have seen

THE NORFOLK DIALECT

The Norfolk dialect has a number of differences in past tense and past participle verb formation from Standard English. In some cases, like *draw*, Standard English irregular verbs are not irregular at all in Norfolk – we say *I drawed*. In other cases, Standard English regular verbs are irregular in Norfolk: for example, the Norfolk past tense of *snow* is *snew*. In yet other cases, partial regularisation has taken place, so that there are two forms instead of three, even though *–ed* is not used, as with *break*; or one form is used instead of two, as with *come* (see below).

Typical Norfolk verb forms include:

present	past	past participle
begin	begun	have begun
beat	beat/bet	have beat/bet
become	become	have become
bite	bit	have bit
blow	blew	have blew
break	broke	have broke
bring	brung	have brung/brought
catch	catched	have catched
choose	chose	have chose
come	come	have come
do	done	have done
draw	drawed	have drawed
drink	drunk	have drunk
drive	driv	have driven
forget	forgot	have forgot
give	give/gan/gon	have give(n)
grow	growed	have growed
know	knowed	have knowed
mow	mew/mowed	have mown

owe	*ewe*	*have own*
ride	*rid*	*have rid(den)*
rise	*ris*	*have ris(en)*
ring	*rung*	*have rung*
run	*run*	*have run*
see	*see*	*have see(n)*
shake	*shook*	*have shook*
show	*shew*	*have shown*
shriok	*shruck*	*have shruck*
snow	*snew*	*have snown*
speak	*spoke*	*have spoke*
steal	*stole*	*have stole*
stink	*stunk*	*have stunk*
swim	*swum*	*have swum*
take	*took*	*have took*
thaw/thow	*thew*	*have thew*
teach	*teached*	*have teached*
tear	*tore*	*have tore*
tread	*trod*	*have trod*
wake	*woke*	*have woke*
wear	*wore*	*have wore*
wrap	*wrop*	*have wrop*
write	*writ*	*have writ*

Some of these forms are very archaic, especially *wrop* and *gon* (the alternative form *gan* appears in *The Boy John Letters*). *Shew*, as the past tense of *show*, is very widely used and is found in the speech even of people whose English is not very dialectal. The past tense of *owe* – *ewe* – is pronounced without any *y* sound at the beginning i.e. not the same as *you*.

Imperatives

Imperatives are verb forms which are used for giving instructions or making orders: *Sit down! Go on! Shut up!* There is an implicit 'you' in such instructions: *(I instruct you to) sit down.* This 'you' is very often made explicit in the Norfolk dialect:

Go you on!

Shut you up!

This is true even when the imperative is strengthened by using the auxiliary verb *do*:

Standard English	Norfolk
Do sit down!	*Do you sit down!*

Individual verbs

● *Be*

○ *Presentative* be

The present tense of the verb *to be* in Norfolk is identical with that in Standard English: *I am, he/she/it is, we/you/they are.* But there is one interesting exception. This concerns the phenomenon which is known as 'presentative *be*'. What this means is that, while people will normally say *I am*, they may nevertheless announce themselves, on arriving somewhere, by saying *Here I be!* Similarly, we usually say *he is*, but if we are looking for someone and find him, we will exclaim *There he be!* That is, *be* is used for all persons when the speaker is presenting themselves or someone or something they have found or come across. These forms probably reflect an earlier stage of the dialect when *be* was the normal present tense form in all meanings, as in parts of the West Country where speakers still say *I be, you be* etc. This is also perhaps why some Norfolk people also say *Right ya be* rather than *Right you are!*

○ *The past tense of* be

The past tense of *to be* is *wus (wooz)* for all persons in the positive, but *weren't* for all persons in the negative:

singular	**plural**
I wus	*we wus*
you wus	*you wus*
he/she/it wus	*they wus*
I weren't	*we weren't*
you weren't	*you weren't*
he/she/it weren't	*they weren't*

The word *weren't* is pronounced in a number of different ways – 'werent, wahnt, wawnt, wonnt' – in different places. The older Norfolk dialect had *wor* rather than *wus* for all persons in the positive.

● *have*

Unless the next word begins with a vowel, *have* is most often pronounced without the final *v*: *Ha'ya got some?* but *Have a look.*

● *Auxiliary and full verb* do

There are two different verbs *to do* in English. One is the full verb *do* which actually refers to 'doing' something. The other is the auxiliary verb *do* which has nothing to do with 'doing' anything and which is used to form questions and negatives, as in *Do you come here often? No, I don't come here often.*

In Norfolk, as in most English dialects, the past tense of full verb *do* is *done* rather than Standard English *did*. However, this is not true of the auxiliary verb *do,* for which the past tense is *did*:

You done it, did you?

It is not at all possible to say *You done it, done you?* Norfolk thus has a grammatical distinction between the full verb and the auxiliary verb which is not found in Standard English.

● dare

The archaic English past tense form of the verb *to dare* was *durst.* In the Norfolk dialect, this has become the present tense form as well:

You dursn't/dussn't = You dare not.

(For more on the pronunciation of words like *dussn't,* see the following chapter.)

In less dialectal local speech, the Standard English negative present tense form, *daren't*, is still distinctive in Norfolk because it is pronounced as two syllables, rhyming with *parent*, unlike in the rest of the country where it is normally pronounced as a single syllable. This is true even of the speech of Norfolk people who otherwise have few regional features in their pronunciation.

● ought

Typical Norfolk forms of this verb, even in the speech of people who otherwise use few dialect forms, include:

You didn't ought to do that, did you?

Did you ought to do that?

rather than the Standard/General forms:

You ought not to do that, ought you?

Ought you to do that?

● *borrow/lend*

As in most other dialects, the word *borrow* occurs only very rarely, and this pair of verbs is not generally distinguished:

> *Can I lend your bike?*

This lack of a distinction is not a problem – it is always clear what is intended. And, indeed, many other languages do not make this distinction at all – the Norwegian verb *låne*, for example, means both 'lend' and 'borrow'.

● *learn/teach*

Similarly, *learn* and *teach* are often not distinguished, with *learn* being used with both meanings:

> *She didn't learn us very good.*

● *matter*

Standard English *It doesn't matter* is most usually *That don't matters* in Norfolk, with an –*s* on the end.

Nouns

Archaic plurals

The older Norfolk dialect had a number of archaic plurals:

house	*housen*
mouse	*meece*

Forby also cites *cheesen* 'cheeses', and *closen* 'clothes'.

Measurement nouns

As in many other dialects, it is common in Norfolk for measurement nouns not to take a plural –s after numerals:

> *four foot*
>
> *three mile*

Telling the time

In telling the time, 25 is *five and twenty*:

> *It's five and twenty past four.*
>
> *The bus come at five and twenty to.*

This is an older usage that was formerly possible in English with all numerals whether in telling the time or not: 'four and thirty', 'five and sixty'.

The definite article

The definite article *the* normally appears in the form *th'* if the next word begins with a vowel:

> *th'old house*
>
> *in th'oven*

In the older dialect, the definite article could be omitted after prepositions of motion and before nouns denoting certain familiar domestic objects:

> *he walked into house*

put th'apples into basket

she come out of barn

kittle boil!

Pronouns

Personal pronouns

The personal pronouns of Standard English are as follows:

singular		plural	
I	*me*	*we*	*us*
you	*you*	*you*	*you*
he	*him*		
she	*her*	*they*	*them*
it	*it*		

● In Norfolk, unstressed *I* is pronounced with a weak vowel ('shwa' – see page 82), even at the end of a sentence, so that *can I?* is pronounced 'canna?' rhyming with *banner*:

    I can't do that, canna?   'I can't do that, can I?'

● In the older dialect, *you* was pronounced to rhyme with *now* and is often spelt *yow* by dialect writers.

● Unstressed *they* is pronounced 'thee':

    Where are thee?   Where are they?

● Stressed *it* in Standard English corresponds to *that* in Norfolk:

    Thass rainen.   = It's raining.

> *That wus me what done it.*   = It was me who did it.

That can also be pronounced without the *th,* especially in Norwich:

> *'Ass rainen.*

In unstressed position, however, *it* does occur:

> *I don't like it, thass no good.*

This use of *that* rather than *it* is something which occurs even in the speech of people who are not strong dialect speakers – very many Norfolk people betray their local origins when they say things like *Hello, that's only me.*

In the older dialect, *thaself* was found rather than *itself:*

> *The dog hurt thaself.*

but this has now disappeared. In the older dialect, *that* also appeared as *ta* or *t':*

> *Ta fruz*   'It froze'.

This has now also disappeared except in the expression *t'is true* 'It's true', as in:

> *I said I wus a-comen, t'is true, but I'm afraid I in't now.*

● Plural *you* is often distinguished from singular *you* through the addition of *together:*

> *Where are you together?*
>
> *Come you on together!*

Together can also occur on its own as a form of plural address:

> *Dinner's ready together!*

Possessive pronouns

The possessive forms *mine, yours, his, hers, ours, theirs* are used to refer to the place where someone lives:

>   *Less go round mine*   = Let's go to my place.

In the older dialect, *your* could be pronounced *yar.*

Reflexive pronouns

In Standard English, the reflexive pronouns are:

myself	ourselves
yourself	yourselves
himself	
herself	themselves
itself	

It can be seen that there is something of an irregularity here, in that some of the forms are based on a combination of *–self* or *–selves* with the possessive pronouns – *myself, yourself, ourselves, yourselves* – while others are based on the *–self* or *–selves* plus the personal pronouns – *himself, themselves.* In Norfolk we do not have this irregularity as the dialect has *hisself, theirselves* instead:

>   *He hart hisself*   'He hurt himself'

Relative pronoun

Standard English has three relative pronouns, *who, which* and *that,* as in:

>   *There's the pen **that** I lost.*

>   *He's the one **who** did it.*

>   *a book **which** I read*

There is only one relative pronoun in Norfolk, *what*

> *There's the pen **what** I lost.*
>
> *He's the one **what** done it.*
>
> *a book **what** I read*

Demonstrative pronouns

The demonstrative pronouns of Standard English are:

	near	distant
singular	this	that
plural	these	those

In Norfolk, the distant plural form is not *those* but *them*. (This is common in very many other dialects too.)

> *Eat you them carrots.* = Eat those carrots.

Very often, these pronouns are reinforced by *here* and *there:*

> *this here book*
>
> *them there books*

There is also an additional form *yin*. This relates to the form *yinder*, which corresponds to the more widely used form 'yonder'. *Yin* is used to refer to something which is even further away than something referred to by *that*. In *The Boy John Letters* we can read things like *Go yow down to yin ind o' this rud* meaning 'Go down to the far end of this road'.

Adjectives

Comparative forms of adjectives have one of two forms: either they end in
–er, like *nicer,* or they take *more* in front of the adjective, like *more interesting.* As in most other dialects, the Norfolk dialect permits double comparatives:

> *This one's more nicer than that one.*

Adverbs

Adverbs versus adjectives

Standard English usually forms adverbs from adjectives by adding *–ly* to
the adjective, as in *loud–loudly,* although some adverbs take a different
form: *good–well.* Like many other dialects, the Norfolk dialect uses the
same form for adjectives and adverbs:

> *She sing nice.*
>
> *He done it good.*

Temporal adverbs

The traditional dialects of Norfolk not only had forms such as *tonight* and
today but also *ta'year, ta'mornen, ta'week,* meaning 'this year', 'this morning', 'this week'.

● *now*

A Norfolk feature found even in the speech of people whose English is not
very dialectal is the use of *now* rather than *just* in expressions such as *I'm
now coming/ I'm now a-comen.*

Intensifiers

The word *wholly*, normally pronounced to rhyme with *woolly*, is often used as an intensifier, like Standard English 'really':

> *That wholly poured!*

Right can also be used in a similar way with adjectives:

> *Ya hatta be right careful.*   'You have to be very careful.'

Another form used in this way is *rare*. This can simply mean 'strange, funny' but it can also be used to intensify the meaning of an adjective:

> *He had rare red fearce.*   'He had a very red face'.

Since *rare* and *real* are pronounced the same (see page 80) except for the *l* at the end of *real*, it is not always clear which word is being used.

Also very distinctive is the (by now old-fashioned) use of *master* as an intensifier with adjectives:

> *That wus master strong.*

Prepositions

As in nonstandard dialects generally, there are many differences in preposition usage between our local dialect and Standard English. Distinctively Norfolk usages include:

*Are you comen **round** John's?*	= **to** John's (place)
*I was **round** John's.*	= **at** John's (place)
*I'm goen **down** the city.*	= **to** Norwich from the suburbs
*I'm goen **up** the city.*	= **to** Norwich from the country

Standard English *of* is usually pronounced as unstressed *a:*

> *a pound a steak*

but is pronounced *on* when stressed or before a vowel:

> *What do you think on it?*

> *There was a couple on 'em.*

The form *alonga,* derived from *along with* or *along of,* is often used in the sense of 'together with':

> *Come you alonga me.*

Conjunctions

do

In the older Norfolk dialect, the word *do* is used as a conjunction which means something like 'otherwise'. The *English Dialect Dictionary* shows that this usage was once found in the dialects of Norfolk, Suffolk, Cambridgeshire and northern Essex. How did this form develop? The answer seems to be that it is an example of what linguists call 'grammaticalisation', in which words increasingly come to be used in a more abstract and grammatical way. Think of these examples from Norfolk dialect literature:

> *Don't you take yours off, do you'll get rheumatism.*

> *Don't you tell your Aunt Agatha about the coupons, do she'll mob me.*

In these examples, the insertion of *because if you* before *do* will provide forms readily comprehensible to speakers of all English dialects:

> *Don't take yours off, [because if you] do you'll get rheumatism.*

It seems, then, that the development of the conjunction *do* began with an initial stage in which speakers simply omitted phrases such as *because if.*

This is not the end of the story, however. A second stage in the development of a more abstract meaning can be illustrated by the following:

> *Have the fox left? No that en't, do Bailey would've let them* [the dogs] *went.*

Here the link between the two parts of the sentence is more abstract and complicated. The originally present tense form *do* is being applied in a past tense context, and *do* is used in spite of the fact that we would have to replace *do* with *had* to get a full version of the sentence:

> *No that en't,* [*because if that had*] *Bailey would've let them went.*

The third and final stage in the process is demonstrated in examples like:

> *That's a good job we come out of that there field, do he'd've had us!*

> *We stabled them elephants right in the middle, do we should've capsized.*

Here present tense *do* is once again being used in past tense contexts, but it is also being used, in spite of the fact that it is a positive verb form, in a situation where a full form of the sentence would require a negative verb and a form of *have* rather than *do*:

> *That's a good job we come out of that there field,* [*because if we hadn't*] *he'd've had us!*

● *time*

The older Norfolk dialect employed *time* as a conjunction in the sense of Standard English *while*:

> *Go you and have a good wash time I git tea ready.*

It is possible that this came from a shortening of *during the time that . . .*

● *(nor) yet*

The form *(nor) yet* may act as a conjunction equivalent to *nor* in sentences such as

> *There weren't no laburnum, yet no lilac.*
>
> *There wouldn't be nothen yet nobody to start things off again.*

● *(no) more*

The form *(no) more* can operate as a conjunction equivalent to *nor* or *neither*:

> *The fruit and vegetables weren't as big as last year, more weren't the taters and onions.*

● *on purpose to*

This is equivalent to General English 'in order to':

> *I went there on purpose to see him.*

('On purpose' in the meaning 'deliberately' is often pronounced *a-parpose: He done it a-parpose.*)

Negation

Multiple negation

In most nonstandard dialects of English, as mentioned in the Introduction, it is usual for all the words in a sentence which can take a negative form to have that negative form:

> *I don't want none.*

This is the well-known 'double negative' that was once found even in Standard English and which occurs in many foreign languages, for example French. 'Multiple negation' is a better term for this, though, because you can certainly have more than two negatives:

> *I couldn't find none nowhere.*

This construction is normal in the Norfolk dialect also. John Kett recognises this, even in poetic lines (from *Pome for Conservation Year)* such as:

> *The Jolly Farmers pub has gone, an' not a stun in't left.*
> = . . . and not a stone isn't left ('and not a stone is left')

A distinctively Norfolk feature is that multiple negation also occurs in sentences with *hardly*:

> *I couldn't find hardly none on'em.*
> = I could find hardly any of them.

in't

The negative form of *be* and *have* in the present tense is *in't* or *en't*, corresponding to the better known form *ain't* used in many other dialects:

> | *I in't comen.* | = I'm not coming. |
> | *They in't teachers.* | = They're not teachers. |
> | *I in't done it yet.* | = I haven't done it yet. |

For some speakers, there is an emphatic form with initial *h:*

> *No, I hin't done it yet!*

Other speakers make a distinction between the negative forms of *be* and *have*.

> *I in't/en't comen.*

I hin't/hen't done it.

It is probable that usage is rather variable here because it has changed and is still changing – Forby describes the 19th-century dialect as having three different forms:

een't	= is not
ain't	= am not
heen't	= have not.

aren't

Some Norfolk people whose speech is not especially dialectal use the form *I aren't* rather than General English *I'm not*. This seems very sensible because, after all, General English does have *aren't I?*

never

As in many other English dialects, the word *never* can be used for past tense negation even for single events:

He never come home last night.

It was never me what broke the window.

THE PRONUNCIATION OF THE NORFOLK DIALECT

In this chapter (and in the recordings at <www.poppyland.co.uk/dialect>) we look at some of the major features of the pronunciation of the Norfolk dialect. We start with some vowel sounds, comparing the Norfolk vowel system with the vowel systems of General English.

Vowels

The Latin alphabet that we use for writing English has only five letters for representing vowel sounds, *a, e, i, o, u* – or six if you include *y.* The problem with this is that English, unlike Latin, has many more than six vowel sounds. The BBC accent has at least 18, and the Norfolk dialect has more than that. In writing about the pronunciation of these vowel sounds, we therefore have to use a system which makes it clear which sounds (as opposed to letters) we are talking about. Following the example of the world's leading authority on English accents, Professor John Wells of London University, I therefore use a system in this book which is designed in such a way that we can always be sure which sound we are referring to. This is a system of 'key words'. For example, one of the key words is KIT. If I refer to 'the KIT vowel', this means that I am talking about the vowel which occurs not only in the word KIT, but also in the complete set of all the very many other words which have this same sound in the English language. That is, the KIT vowel is the short *i* found in hundreds of other words such as *bid, tip, kiss, Jim, bitten, women* and so on, not all of which are necessarily spelled with the letter *i*. The THOUGHT vowel is the vowel sound which occurs in *thought, law, Laura, ball, caught*. The FLEECE vowel is the one which occurs in *fleece, meat, Pete, meet, be* – and so on.

The short e vowel

Some words which have the DRESS vowel – the 'short *e* vowel' that occurs in *dress* – in General English have the KIT vowel instead in Norfolk. This is particularly true if *t* or *d* follow the vowel:

General English	Norfolk
get	*git*
kettle	*kittle*
thread	*trid*
head	*hid*
yet	*yit*
ready	*riddy*
yes	*yis*

On the other hand, before *v* and *th,* the TRAP vowel is found:

never	*navver*
together	*togather*
weather	*wather*
several	*savveral*

This is also true of a number of other words:

better	*batter*
letter	*latter*
yellow	*yalla*

71

The short *o* vowel

The LOT vowel of words such as *top, bottom, hot, cod, Tom* etc is pronounced without rounding the lips and sounds rather like the vowel used by Americans in these words. *Lot* sounds a bit like 'laht', only shorter.

The negative prefix *un-* is also pronounced with this vowel: *on-tie* 'untie'; and so are *onder* 'under' and *onderneath* 'underneath'.

The NURSE vowel

One of the most distinctive features of the older Norfolk dialect is that the vowel we find in most forms of English in England in words like *nurse, bird, church, girl* does not occur. What happens instead can be seen by looking at literature written in the Norfolk dialect, such as *The Boy John Letters*. The author, Sidney Grapes, used spellings in his letters for some NURSE words like these:

word	dialect spelling
her	*har*
heard	*hard*
nerves	*narves*
herself	*harself*
service	*sarvice*
earn	*arn*
early	*arly*
concern	*consarn*
sir	*sar*
fur	*far*

Here it can be seen that words spelt with *ear* and *er* are represented as having *ar* in the dialect. So are words spelt with *ir* and *ur* where these come at the end of the word. These words, then, did not have the NURSE vowel but the vowel of START. So *sir* rhymed with *car,* and *fur* and *far* were pronounced the same. Even in the modern dialect, men called Herbert may be affectionately called *Harbo* or, in Norwich, *Arbo.* This development was once widespread in England, and led to some permanent changes in the language: *person* and *parson,* for example, were originally the same word; and a number of words, such as *heart,* have kept this pronunciation in all forms of English. Norfolk place-names, too, were affected: *Barningham* used to be *Berningham.*

In certain other words, on the other hand, we find spellings in *The Boy John Letters* like:

word	dialect spelling
first	*fust, fasst*
worse	*wuss*
church	*chuch, chatch*
purpose	*pappus*
turnip	*tannip*
further	*futher*
hurl	*hull*
turkey	*takkey*
turn	*tann*
hurting	*hatten*
nightshirt	*niteshat*
shirts	*shats*
girl	*gal*

This is a purely local dialect development. Here we find mostly words which are spelt with *ir* and *ur* where they do not occur at the end of a word. Notice that Sidney Grapes sometimes spells these with *a* and sometimes with *u,* so that *church* can appear as *chuch* or *chatch.* The reason for this is that these words are pronounced with a vowel which does not exist in General English and which we have no letter for. The vowel is neither the vowel of TRAP nor the vowel of STRUT but something in between. So the word *turn* is pronounced with a vowel sound intermediate between that of *tan* and *tun*.

On the subject of words such as this in East Anglian dialects, Forby (page 92) wrote:

> To the syllable *ur* (and consequently to *ir* and *or*, which have often the same sound) we give a pronunciation certainly our own.
>
> Ex. *Third word burn curse*
>
> *Bird curd dirt worse*

> It is one which can be neither intelligibly described, nor represented by other letters. It must be heard. Of all legitimate English sounds, it seems to come nearest to *open a* [the vowel of *balm*], or rather to the rapid utterance of the *a* in the word *arrow*, supposing it to be caught before it light on the *r . . . Bahd* has been used to convey our sound of *bird*. Certainly this gets rid of the danger of *r;* but the *h* must as certainly be understood to lengthen the sound of *a;* which is quite inconsistent with our snap-short utterance of the syllable. In short it must be heard.

days vs. *daze*

In Norfolk we have two different vowels corresponding to the single long *a* FACE vowel of General English. This is because all forms of English used to have two such vowels up until the 17th century, but most dialects have now lost the difference between the two, while we have kept it. It is mostly possible to tell which word has which of the two vowels by looking at the spelling. This is because the spelling reflects the original Middle English pronunciation.

In Norfolk, words like *day, may, pay, praise, maid, raise, eight, weight, wait,* which are spelt with *ay, ai* or *ei*, are pronounced with a diphthong, a vowel which begins with one sound and ends with another. Our vowel in *day* sounds rather as if it begins with the TRAP vowel and ends with the FLEECE vowel, and it is not very different from the way these words are pronounced in other parts of southern England.

On the other hand, words which are spelt with *a_e*, like *gate, face, tape, lake, safe*, are pronounced with a pure vowel (a monophthong). This vowel is rather similar to the one used in these words in many of the dialects of Lancashire and Yorkshire. Norfolk dialect writers normally spell it with *ear* or *air*: 'fearce' = *face*, but this spelling is rather confusing for outsiders, particularly people like Scots or Americans who pronounce the *r* in words like *fear*. John Kett uses *aa* – 'faace'. Perhaps the best way to describe the vowel to people who have not heard it is to say that it is rather like the DRESS vowel, only longer. So *gate* is pronounced rather like a longer version of *get*. (In the older dialect, this same vowel could also be heard in some words spelt with *ea*, such as *creature, dead, eat, ease, please, cheat,* and *bean.*)

In the Norfolk dialect, then, pairs of words like the following are *not* pronounced the same, although they are in most other forms of English:

monophthong	diphthong
daze	days
made	maid
wade	weighed
gaze	gays
gate	gait
graze	greys
pale	pail
male	mail
place	plaice
sale	sail
tale	tail

Nowadays, this distinction between the two vowels is being lost, and most younger people use the diphthong in both sets of words, so that *daze* now sounds the same as *days.* This has led to an interesting development. There are some people who are very fond of the Norfolk dialect and who want to speak or write in as Norfolk a way as possible but who have never mastered the original distinction between these two vowels. These people not only try to pronounce *daze* with the pure vowel but sometimes erroneously pronounce *days* in the same way as well. This is particularly common, too, in dialect writing, unfortunately. There are people who try to write in the Norfolk dialect but who use incorrect spellings such as *dairze* for *days* and *plaired* for *played*. These are mistakes of a kind which is called 'hyperdialectism' – trying to speak or write the dialect but overdoing it!

If people want to see how to write the Norfolk dialect, they should follow the example of Sidney Grapes, who observed this distinction scrupulously. He writes, for example:

monophthongs	diphthongs
pearper for paper, but	*neybors* for neighbours
plearces places	*gays*
learbor labour	*say*
pleartes plates	*days*
keark cake	*straight*
fearce face	*lay*

In one of his letters, he writes: *Old Mrs W— wus full o' earkes and pains.* The word 'ache' is shown as having the monophthong, while 'pain' has the diphthong. To write 'pain' as **pairn* or **pearn* would have been quite wrong, something which modern dialect writers would do well to remember!

nose vs. *knows*

In Norfolk we have two different vowels corresponding to the single long *o* GOAT vowel of General English. This is, once again, because all forms of English used to have two such vowels up until the 17th century, but most dialects have now lost the difference between the two, while we have kept it. It is, again, mostly possible to tell which word has which of the two vowels by looking at the spelling.

Words spelt with *ou, ow* and *ol* like *soul, know, told* are pronounced rather like they are much of the rest of southern England, with a noticeable diphthong. This sounds rather as if it starts with the vowel of STRUT and ends with the vowel of *school*.

On the other hand, long *o* words which are spelt with *oa* or *o_e* or just *o*, such as *coal, hope, most,* have a very different and distinctive Norfolk vowel which to many outsiders sounds very like the long *u* sound of LOOSE but which is in fact not the same. It is pronounced further back in the mouth and is very similar to the sound of *ou* in French *nous* 'we' and the long sound of *u* in German *gut* 'good'.

This means that in Norfolk, pairs of words such as the following are not pronounced the same, unlike in most other forms of English:

monophthong	diphthong
sole	*soul*
nose	*knows*
road	*rowed* (as in *rowed* a boat)
groan	*grown*
moan	*mown*
so	*sew*
toe	*tow*
throes	*throws*

The title of the Beatles' 1970s album used a pun, *Rubber Soul,* which does not work in the Norfolk dialect. And writing *IOU* for *I owe you* does not work in Norfolk either, because the name of the letter *o* and the word *owe* are not pronounced the same. The Norfolk dialect, we can say, has one more vowel here than other varieties of English.

This vowel distinction is still alive and well in the local dialect, and much 'healthier' than the *daze/days* distinction. Generally, the only people who make a mistake of the hyperdialectism kind with these vowels are outsiders who try to imitate the Norfolk dialect and wrongly say things like **Loostoft* for *Lowestoft* and **oon* for *own*.

There is a complication, though, with the word *no*. For older speakers, *no* has the same vowel as *nose*, but younger people pronounce it the same as *know* except when it is an adverb, so that in *No, thass no good,* the first *no* rhymes with *low*, and the second one with *so!*

Note also that in the older dialect *hoe* and *mole* were pronounced with the diphthong and not with the monophthong as the spelling would suggest.

The East Anglian short *o*

Another well known feature of the Norfolk dialect, and of some neighbouring areas, is the 'East Anglian short *o*'. This term refers to the pronunciation of words from the left-hand column, above, i.e. long *o* words such as *road, loaf, coat, whole, home, comb, bone, stone, loke, throat,* and *goat*. In the Norfolk dialect these words, if they end in a consonant-sound like *road* or *nose* (but not if they end with a vowel like *so*), can also be pronounced with the vowel of FOOT. This means that *road* can rhyme with *good, loke* can rhyme with *book,* and *throat* and *goat* can rhyme with *put*. This is still very much a feature of living speech, so that even relatively new words can have this feature. For instance, the *Hippodrome* theatre in Norwich had this vowel in the last syllable of its name; and *Kodachrome* has it in its first and last syllables.

The word *don't* comes into this class of words, too, but it can also be pronounced as *dawnt*.

Yod-dropping

General English words spelt with *ue, u_e,* and *ew,* such as *music, new, pew, tune, queue, Bute, due, few, huge, view* are actually pronounced with a *y* sound after the first consonant and before the long *u* (or LOOSE vowel), so that *Bute* is pronounced 'Byute'. In Norfolk this *y* has gone missing, so that *Bute* can be identical with *boot,* and *Hugh* and *who* are pronounced the same. So are *due, dew* and *do*. This is known as 'yod-dropping', *yod* being the name for the *y* sound.

Words spelt with *oo*

The FOOT vowel also occurs in the words *roof, proof, hoof*. (In most other English accents these words are pronounced with the LOOSE vowel.) Also, in Norfolk the plurals of these words are *hoofs* etc. and not *hooves* etc.

Many Norfolk people also pronounce *room, broom* with the FOOT vowel rather than the LOOSE vowel.

In the older dialect, some words like *soot, roof* were pronounced with the STRUT vowel, so that *roof* was identical with *rough*.

However, most LOOSE words which are spelt with *oo* (plus one or two other words such as *move*) behave in a rather complicated way. In the true Norfolk dialect these words have the same vowel as the words like *new, tune, due* that we just discussed under 'yod-dropping', as well as other *u_e* words such as *rude, rule, lute*, so that *loot* and *lute* are the same. However, for very many people with more modern accents, some or many of these words are pronounced with the same Norfolk long *o* vowel as *so, groan, toe*, as described above. For example, *boot* in the old dialect is pronounced the same as *Bute* (without the *y*, of course). Many modern speakers, however, pronounce it the same as *boat*. This means that pairs of words like these may be identical in pronunciation:

> *fool*　　*foal*
>
> *moon*　　*moan* (which is not the same as *mown*)
>
> *boot*　　*boat*
>
> *move*　　*mauve*

and that *school* and *rule* do not rhyme. (Some words in this class, however, never cross over to the *boat* set: *loose* and *soon*, for example.)

This is all rather confusing. Let us sum it up, bringing in the not very common word *rood*, meaning 'cross' as found in a church, like this:

In the Norfolk dialect, there are three different vowels in the word-sets *rude – road – rowed* because we preserve the historical Middle English distinction between the last two. (General English has only two vowels at this point, one for *rude – rood* and the other for *road – rowed*.) Thus, in Norfolk:

- Words like *rude* are always pronounced with the LOOSE vowel.

- Words like *rood* can be pronounced with the LOOSE vowel **or** with the distinctive Norfolk vowel we described above as being like French *ou*.

- Words like *road* can be pronounced either with the distinctive Norfolk vowel we described above as being like French *ou*, **or** with the vowel of FOOT and *good*.

- Words like *rowed* are different from *road*.

here vs. *hair*

We do not distinguish between the vowels of SQUARE and NEAR in the Norfolk dialect. The single vowel that we do have is more like the General English pronunciation of the SQUARE vowel. This means that *here* and *there* rhyme, and that the following pairs of words are identical:

beer	*bear*
cheer	*chair*
deer, dear	*dare*
ear	*air*
fear	*fair*
here, hear	*hair*
leer	*lair*
mere	*mare*
pier, peer	*pare, pear*
rear	*rare*
really	*rarely*
sheer	*share*
sneer	*snare*
steer	*stare*

tear	*tear*
we're, weir	*wear, ware*
year	*Yare*

Note that *idea* is the same as *I dare*, *creosote* sounds like 'crairsote', and *vehicle* like 'vaircle'.

sure and *pure*

In the modern dialect, the words *cure, endure, fury, furious, jury, lure, Muriel, pure, sure, you're* are not pronounced with the vowel of THOUGHT as they are in many kinds of English but with the vowel of NURSE. This is true even of very non-dialectal speech, so that *sure* rhymes with *her*. Because of yod-dropping, this also has the consequence that the following pairs of words are pronounced the same:

purr	*pure*
cur	*cure*
furry	*fury*

The names of the River *Bure* and *Ber* Street in Norwich are also pronounced the same.

off and *cloth*

Words such as *cough, off, scoff, soft, broth, cloth, froth, moth, cost, frost, loss, lost, wasp* are pronounced not with the vowel of LOT but with the vowel of THOUGHT: 'cawff, brawth, lawst' etc. This is especially common in *off*, pronounced in Norfolk as 'awff'. Also, the word *dog* is 'dawg', and *job* can be 'jawb'.

Shwa

The most common vowel in English is called 'shwa'. In spite of the fact that it is so common, we have no letter in the alphabet to represent it. It is the vowel which occurs in the first syllable of *ahead, ago, away* and in the second syllable of *China, matter, reckon, rhythm*. This vowel is even more common in the Norfolk dialect than in other forms of English. We tend to have it in unstressed syllables where other dialects have the short *i* KIT vowel. If I represent shwa by writing *uh*, then Norfolk speakers do not say *America* as 'uhmericuh' like in other dialects but 'uhmeruhcuh'. We do not pronounce *wanted* as 'wantid' but 'wantuhd'. We say *David* and *naked* as 'Davuhd' and 'nakuhd'. The pronoun *I* can have this vowel, too, so that *can I?* rhymes with *banner,* as we saw earlier. (Strangely enough, however, some people say *Norfick* and *Suffick*.)

For many words ending in *-y,* older people still say 'veruh', 'monuh', 'cituh' instead of *very, money, city,* often represented by dialect writers as *verra* etc. – *The Boy John Letters* often refer to village characters such as *Billa* and *Jimma*.

Like people in many other parts of the country, we also pronounce *barrow, window* etc. as 'barruh', 'winduh'.

It is also a distinctive feature of the rhythm of Norfolk speech that stressed syllables tend to be longer than in other kinds of English. This means that unstressed syllables with shwa can disappear altogether:

forty two	>	'fooort' two'
Have you got any money?	>	'Haa'ya got'na munna?'
quarter to five	>	'quaar't'five'

Smoothing

When shwa follows certain other vowels, it can combine with them to produce some distinctively Norfolk results which go by the name of 'smoothing'. For example, the LOOSE vowel of words like *new, two, do* followed by shwa turns into the NURSE vowel:

do it = do + 'uht' > 'durt'

which means that *do it* and *dirt* are pronounced the same.

Also the FACE vowel plus shwa turns into a longer version of the TRAP vowel, so that *playing* sounds like *plan*, only longer, and *Heigham* (as in *Heigham Street* in Norwich) sounds like a longer version of *ham*.

In the same way, the vowel of *boat, go* plus shwa turns into the THOUGHT vowel, so that *going* is pronounced *gawn*; and the FLEECE vowel plus shwa turns into the SQUARE vowel, so that *seeing* rhymes with *cairn*.

Interestingly, the same thing that happens to *seeing* also happens to *we've*. The word *have* is typically pronounced without the *v* in Norfolk (see page 55), so that *we have* is reduced in speech, not to *we've* as in General English, but to *we*+ 'uh', which gives 'wair'. As we saw on page 81, *we're* is also pronounced 'wair' in Norfolk, so that *we have* and *we are* end up being pronounced the same:

We have done it	'Wair done uht'
We are going	'Wair gawn'

Smoothing is a feature which currently appears to be spreading outwards form Norfolk, southwards and westwards into other regions.

Consonants

h-dropping

Most local accents in England and Wales have *h*-dropping – speakers sometimes, often, or always do not pronounce the *h* in words like *hammer, hill, house*. There are two areas of England, however, where this has traditionally not been true. These are the Northeast and East Anglia. The traditional Norfolk dialect kept its *h*s. The Norwich version of the dialect, however, has had *h*-dropping for well over a hundred years – this was, until at least the 1960s, the best way of telling a country person from a city person. However, this is not now so easy, as *h*-dropping has begun to spread into the surrounding countryside from the city. Even so, *h*-dropping is not nearly as common in Norwich as it is, say, in London, Leeds or Birmingham.

The *v/w* merger

The older Norfolk dialect had a very interesting feature that was once found all over the southeast of England, including London, and probably survived longer in Norfolk than anywhere else. This was the pronunciation of *v* as *w* where it occurred at the beginning of a stressed syllable in words such as *very, vegetable, village, averse*. Words with *v* in other positions, such as *love, move, every*, were not affected. This feature appears to have died out of widespread, spontaneous, natural usage during the 1920s. It is therefore very interesting that this feature is still remembered by Norfolk people, including dialect writers, who continue to write things like *werry, anniwarsery, willage* long after people stopped actually using this pronunciation except as a joke.

hundred and *naked*

A very distinctive feature of the Norfolk dialect which can still be heard is the pronunciation of *d* as *t* in unstressed syllables at the end of a word. So *hundred, naked* and *David* are all pronounced with a final *t*. The name *David* in Norfolk thus differs in three ways from the way it is pronounced in General English: they say 'Dayvid', while we say 'Dairvuht' (for the vowels, see pages 75 and 82 above).

Glottal stops

There are three different ways of pronouncing *t* in Norfolk when it occurs at the end of a word, as in *bet*, or at the end of a syllable as in *better, bottle*.

First, it can be pronounced like the *t* in other positions, as in *tea*, using the front of the tongue.

Second, it can be pronounced in the throat as a glottal stop. This is the pronunciation usually indicated in writing as *be'er* and is sometimes called 'dropping your *t*s'. (This is not a good name for it, since of course the *t* is not dropped at all – it is just pronounced in a different way. If you drop the *t* from *fleeting,* you get *fleeing*, not *flee'ing*.) In words like *twenty, plenty* the *n* is dropped before the glottal stop: 'twe'y'.

The glottal stop is a perfectly normal consonant and occurs in many of the world's languages. It is found in most varieties of English in England, and is not at all unique to Norfolk, although there is some evidence that it may have started in our county and spread from there to the rest of the country: a major dialect survey carried out in the 1950s showed it to be more common in Norfolk than nearly anywhere else.

The third pronunciation is more typical of our region. This is where the *t* is pronounced with the tip of the tongue and as a glottal stop simultaneously. This is difficult to describe, but people who are not familiar with this Norfolk pronunciation may know it from the northeastern Geordie accent or from Belfast, where it is also common. The same sort of thing can happen to *p* and *k* where they occur between two vowels, as in *taper, baker*. In pronouncing the *p* in *taper*, for instance, we pronounce the *p* by closing our lips and making a glottal stop at the same time.

Clear *l*

Most forms of English in England have two different *l* sounds. You can hear this clearly in a word like *little*, in which, if you listen carefully, you will notice that the second *l* is different from the first. The first one has a clear or thin sound, while the second one is 'darker'. In the older Norfolk dialect, however, this is not the case. The *l* sound where it occurs at the end of *little,* and generally after a vowel in words like *hill, milk,* is pronounced with the same clear or thin *l* sound which occurs at the beginning of words. This is also the case in Irish English and in the speech, for instance, of people who speak English with a French accent. Younger people in Norfolk no longer have this pronunciation, however.

thr and *shr*

In the older Norfolk dialect, *shr* and *thr* at the beginning of words are pronounced *sr* and *tr:*

	Norfolk pronunciation
shriek	'sriek'
shrimp	'srimp'
thread	'trid'
throat	'troot' (rhyming with *foot*)
threshing	'troshen'
threshold	'troshel'

(My own family name seems to be a Norfolk form of Threadgold.)

glass and *class*

In the older dialect, words beginning with *gl* and *cl* could be pronounced with *tl* and *dl*: *glove* 'dlove', *clock* 'tlock'.

Individual words

Here is a short list of words which have different pronunciations in Norfolk from that in other places:

across	'acrawst'
after	'ahter'
against	'agin'
always	'olluz'
awkward	'awkard'

before	'afore'
boil	'bile'
boy	'boo-y'
catch	'ketch'
enough	'enow'
horse	'hoss'
marsh	'maysh'
nothing	'nothen' with the vowel of LOT, not STRUT
old	'owd'
only	'oony'
quarter	'corter'
shoulder, bowl	have the vowel of MOUTH and not of *know*
shed	'shud'
shut	'shet'
sit	'set'
such	'sitch'
thought	'thowt' (with the vowel of *know*)
won't, wouldn't	'oon't'
yesterday	'yisty'

In the older dialect, words ending in *–ly* could be pronounced with *–lie: accorden-lie* 'accordingly'.

Place-names

People coming to Norfolk for the first time have to learn that we always say Yarmouth and Dereham and not Great Yarmouth or East Dereham, and that streets in Norwich which are named after saints are never called 'street', so we do not say St Stephen's Street or St Augustine's Street or St Giles' Street but St Stephen's, St Augustine's and St Giles. But the biggest problem they face has to do with the pronunciation of the names of our towns and villages. Everybody should know that Norwich is pronounced 'Norridge', to rhyme with *porridge*; and the famously difficult place-names are Costessey, which is pronounced 'Cossy'; Happisburgh, which is 'Hayzbruh', and Wymondham, which is 'Wind'm'.

Wymondham.

Apart from these, there are a number of other difficult place names, the pronunciation of which all Norfolk people are agreed about (the stress is on the part in capital letters where it is not obvious):

Spelled:	Pronounced:
Acle	Aycle
Ashmanhaugh	ASHm'no
Aslacton	AzLACt'n
Belaugh	Beeluh
Bergh Apton	BerAPT'n
Colney	Coaney
Corpusty	CORpuhsty
Deopham	Deep'm
Elsing	Elz'n
Fulmodestone	FULLmuhst'n

Great Hautbois common.

Gimingham	Gim'n'm (with a 'hard g')
Haveringland	Havverl'nd
Hautbois	HUBBuhss
Hellesdon	Helzd'n
Keswick	Kezzick
Matlaske	Matluhsk
Postwick	Pozzick
Potter Heigham	High'm
Rushall	Ruesh'll
Sall	Saul
Shotesham	Shots'm
Sprowston	Sprowst'n (with the vowel of *old*, not *out*)
Stody	Studdy
Swardeston	Swaw(d)st'n
Tacolneston	Tackle-st'n
Tivetshall	Tivvets'll
Walsingham	Wolz'n'm

Wickmere	Wickmuh
Wortwell	Wuttle

Then there are names which we don't all agree about. The disagreement comes from the fact that many place-names now have new *spelling pronunciations*. This is a feature which is by no means confined to place-names. Quite a lot of English words acquired spelling pronunciations during the course of the 20th century, as people who were worried about being 'correct' in their pronunciation (so usually not the aristocracy or upper classes!) looked to spelling for a guide as to how words 'ought' to be pronounced, and stopped using the natural, original pronunciations. Everybody, for example, used to pronounce *handkerchief* 'hankercha', and *waistcoat* was 'weskit'. Similarly, everyone used to call Ipswich 'Ipsidge', but we no longer do so. With Norfolk place names, then, a good guide is that the pronunciation which is most *unlike* the spelling is the original one, and the one which is more like the spelling is a newer one which has come into being as a result of people feeling insecure about their speech. In the following list, I present place-names together with their older pronunciations which, however, are not used by everyone any more, or in some cases, probably, by anyone at all.

Spelled	Pronounced
Aylsham	Ells'm/Ellsh'm
Cley	Clay
Coltishall	Colts'll (with *Colt*- rhyming with *bolt*)
Crostwick	Crossick
Foulsham	Fowlss'm/Fowlsh'm (with *Fowl*- rhyming with *soul*)
Garboldisham	Garb'lss'm/Garb'lsh'm
Hoveton	Hofft'n
Hunstanton	Hunst'n
Letheringsett	Larnsuhtt
Martham	Mart'm
Northrepps	Nurrepps

Salhouse	Selluhss
Southery	Suddery
Southrepps	Surrepps
Stiffkey	Stewkey
Trowse	Trouse (rhyming with *mouse*)
Walsham (N. & S.)	Wolss'm
Weybourne	Webb'n
Wiveton	Wiff'n

Most people in the Norwich area now pronounce *Trowse* with the vowel of *know*, but the original form of the name was *tre-hus* meaning 'wooden house', and Old English *hus* has of course become *house.*

The cases of place-names such as Walsham and Martham are particularly interesting. From what we said on pages 16-17 and 22 about Old English names ending in *-ham*, it will be clear that originally these places would have been *Wals-ham* and *Mart-ham*, so that using *sh* and *th* sounds in these names is historically wrong. Reepham, however, used to be spelt Reefham, and so the *f/ph* sound here is historically correct.

Forby tells us that, in the early nineteenth century, Norfolk people used to pronounce the *g* in phrases like 'bring it' i.e. *bring- git,* rather as people from Birmingham and Liverpool do to this day, except that in Norfolk the *g* was only pronounced if a vowel followed. There is no trace of this left in the Norfolk dialect, except that place names containing *–ing* can be – or at least could be until recently – pronounced in this same way, e.g.:

Spelled	**Pronounced**
Sheringham	Shering-gam
Trimingham	Triming-gam

THE NORFOLK DIALECT IN THE WORLD

Earlier, we discussed the development of the English language after the arrival of the Anglo-Saxon peoples on our coasts in the 5th century. By the 8th century, English was spoken in nearly all of England, as well as in southern and eastern Scotland. Since that time it has gradually increased its presence in the British Isles, so that it is now spoken even in areas where the Celtic languages were spoken longest – Cornwall, Wales, northwestern Scotland, and Ireland, although Scottish and Irish Gaelic still survive, and the Welsh language is doing very well.

This is not the only form of expansion which the English language has undergone, however. Since the 17th century it has spread as a native language to other continents in other parts of the world. We have already noted that the Norfolk dialect played an important part in the formation of Standard English. We can now see that it has also played a significant role in the development of some of these overseas, colonial varieties of English.

Of course, no American today sounds as if he or she came from Norfolk. But there are features of American English which are clearly traceable back over 400 years to an origin in Norfolk. If you look at a map of that area of the northeastern United States which is known as New England – the states of Maine, Massachusetts, Connecticut, Rhode Island, Vermont and New Hampshire – you will see that people from Norfolk must have played quite a big role in the settlement of this area. New England is full of towns with names like Norwich, Attleboro, Yarmouth, Framingham, Walpole, Rockland, Hingham, Lynn, and even Norfolk itself. Puritanism was a potent force in 17th-century Norfolk, and the Pilgrim Fathers included many migrants from our area.

This had some clear linguistic consequences. On page 78 we discussed the feature known as the East Anglian short *o*. This label refers to the pronunciation of words like *road, stone* with the vowel of FOOT. The English dialects of eastern New England also have a short *o*. It does not work exactly like the East Anglian feature, as *boat* and *foot* do not rhyme. Instead, *road, boat* etc have a vowel which is shorter than the normal long *o* vowel, but it is different both from the vowel of FOOT and the vowel of LOT. It is probable that this was the situation in East Anglia also at an earlier period, and that the merger of the vowel in these words with the vowel of FOOT was a later development which occurred in East Anglia but not in New England, so that the American dialect reflects a more conservative stage of this change than our dialect.

We also saw on page 78 that the Norfolk dialect is characterised by yod-dropping – the pronunciation of words like *beautiful* without a *y* sound, so that *who* and *Hugh* are pronounced the same. Most forms of northern United States and Canadian English also have yod-dropping, although this is not as extensive as in Norfolk. They have yod-dropping after *t, d* and *n*, but not after *m, p, b, c, f, v* like Norfolk does. So Americans and Canadians agree with us in having no *y* in words like *new, nude, nuisance, tune, tube, Tuesday, attitude, student, due, dew, dune, duke.* Probably, once again, they are a little more conservative than us and have not taken this trend to its full conclusion.

It is possibly the influence of our form of English which has also led to many Americans, unlike most English people, having the NURSE vowel in words like *cure, endure, fury, furious, jury, lure, pure, sure, you're* instead of the vowel of THOUGHT, so that *rural* rhymes with *referral* and not *choral.*

And the influence of the Norfolk dialect has not been confined simply to North America. One of the features on which we concentrated on pages 82 was the presence of the shwa vowel *uh* in unstressed syllables in Norfolk where other dialects have the short *i* vowel of KIT. We are not alone in the world, however, in having *uh* in *naked*: 'nakuhd' rather than 'nakid'. Australian and New Zealand English also have this characteristic, and it is very likely that this is the result, at least in part, of our kind of English having been one of the inputs to the mixture of dialects that existed in these countries after the early migrations and before the development out of these mixtures of the distinctive forms of English that are spoken there now.

Our pronunciation of *v* as *w* has also left its mark on varieties of English around the world. The English of the Bahamas and some of the Caribbean islands still have this pronunciation, and we can imagine that East Anglian sailors may have played some part in this.

And the influence of our dialect has not been confined to pronunciation. One aspect of Norfolk grammar, the third-person singular zero form as in *he go*, has been much discussed by linguists interested in African American Vernacular English (AAVE) – the English of many Black Americans – and why it is different from the English of White Americans. AAVE also has this feature, and one group of linguists who believed that the origins of AAVE lie mainly in the dialects of the British Isles suggested an origin in East Anglia. Most people now think, however, that the resemblance between AAVE and East Anglian dialect is a kind of coincidence. On page 50, we suggested that our *he go*-type forms were the result of the influence of the Strangers and the fact that they were speaking English as a foreign language. Many linguists now believe that the AAVE phenomenon can be explained in the same sort of way, since obviously the ancestors of modern Black Americans came from Africa and did not speak English natively either.

But one aspect of Norfolk grammar has certainly travelled beyond our shores. The conjunction *do* is not found anywhere in the British Isles outside East Anglia. Nor, as far as I know, is it found anywhere else in the English-speaking world, with one exception – the southeastern United States. One informant for the *Dictionary of American Regional English* (DARE) writes that in eastern North Carolina, during the period approximately from 1915 to 1930,

> I remember hearing White people, speakers with moderate education, saying things like 'Shut the door tight, do it'll blow open before morning' and 'Leave the note in the middle of the table, do she won't see it'.

It would be reasonable to assume that conjunction *do* arrived in North Carolina in the speech of immigrants from East Anglia. It also occurs in the speech of African Americans in northern Florida, as portrayed in the novels of Zora Neal Hurston. Hurston was born in Eatonville, Florida, the first incorporated Black town in the United States, in 1903. Here are some examples:

Dat's a thing dat's got to be handled just so, do it'll kill you. (*Mules and Men,* 1935)

You got to have a subjick tuh talk from, do you can't talk. (*Their Eyes,* 1937)

Git this spoon betwixt her teeth do she's liable to bite her tongue off. (*Seraph,* 1948)

BIBLIOGRAPHY

Jacek Fisiak & Peter Trudgill (eds.), *East Anglian English* (Woodbridge: Boydell & Brewer, 2001)

Robert Forby, *The Vocabulary of East Anglia* (1830; reprinted New York: Augustus M. Kelley, 1970). 2 vols

Sidney Grapes, *The Boy John Letters* (Norwich: Wensum Books, 1974)

John Kett, *Tha's a Rum'un Tew!: Norfolk Verse* (Woodbridge: Baron Publishing, 1975)

Robert Malster, *The Mardler's Companion* (Holbrook: Malthouse Press, 1999)

Jonathan Mardle, *Broad Norfolk* (1958; Norwich: Wensum Books, 1973)

Karl Inge Sandred & Bengt Lindström, *The Place-names of Norfolk I: The Place-names of the City of Norwich* (Nottingham: English Place-Name Society, 1989)

Karl Inge Sandred, *The Place-names of Norfolk II: The Hundreds of East and West Flegg, Happing and Tunstead.* (Nottingham: English Place-Name Society, 1996)

Keith Skipper, *Larn Yarself Norfolk: A Comprehensive Guide to the Norfolk Dialect* (Toftwood: Nostalgia Publications, 1996)

Peter Trudgill, *The Social Differentiation of English in Norwich* (Cambridge University Press, 1974)

Peter Trudgill, *The Dialects of England* (Oxford: Basil Blackwell, 1999)

J. C. Wells, *Accents of English* (Cambridge University Press, 1982). 3 vols

Websites

Friends of Norfolk Dialect: <www.norfolkdialect.com>

Poppyland Publishing: <www.poppyland.co.uk/dialect> includes sound recordings pepared by Peter Trudgill exemplifying some of the features described in this book.

INDEX